Anne Rankin Mahoney

Juvenile Justice
in Context

Northeastern University Press
Boston

Northeastern University Press
Copyright © 1987 Anne Rankin Mahoney

Library of Congress Cataloging-in-Publication Data

Mahoney, Anne Rankin.
  Juvenile justice in context.

  Bibliography: p.
  Includes index.
  1. Juvenile justice, Administration of—United States.
2. Juvenile courts—United States.   I. Title.
HV9104.M22   1987   364.3'6'0973   87–1710
ISBN 1–55553–011–7 (alk. paper)

Printed in the United States of America
91 90 89 88 87   5 4 3 2 1

This book was composed in Gill Sans and Bembo by Crane Typesetting Service, Inc.
Barnstable, Mass. It was printed and bound by Edwards Brothers, Inc., Ann Arbor,
Michigan. The paper is Glatfelter Antique Natural, an acid-free sheet.

For All The Children

Table of Contents

Figures and Tables

Acknowledgments

The individuals who worked in Suburban Court and all its related agencies made this book possible. I would never have thought about writing it without their willingness to share their work, their commitment to children, and their desire to see the system improve. Two juvenile court judges were especially helpful and without their support and permission at preliminary stages, we could not have conducted our research. I hope I have honored their commitment to justice and to children throughout. I would like to thank many people by name, but cannot without violating the confidentiality we have tried so hard to maintain. Any errors are my responsibility, and the book's perspective is my own. It does not necessarily reflect the opinions of anyone in Suburban Court.

The research on which this book was based was primarily supported by the Office of Juvenile Justice and Delinquency Prevention, U.S. Department of Justice, grant number 79–JN–AX–0034. The research on juveniles in municipal courts was supported by a grant from the Academic Research Center of the University of Denver.

Dr. William Key, who was chair of the Department of Sociology and director of the Academic Research Center while I was working on this project, supported it by creating an environment in which research was encouraged and valued. Carol Fenster was the field supervisor for the research project that provided the basis for this book. She is a highly gifted field worker, supervisor, and sociologist. Her skill contributed immeasurably to our ongoing good relationship with court personnel and the quality of the research. Ken Seeley played an important role in commencing the larger research project, of which

x   this study was a part. Timothy B. Walker helped us think through potential legal problems. Steve Harvey, Louis Propp, and Jana Waters worked as research assistants in the court agencies and provided insights into court operations. Others who contributed in major ways to the project's court data collection efforts include Sue Bozinovski, Joyce Freeman, Anne Harper, and Susan Stuber. Jenny Huang and Jessica Kohout kept track of data files and handled quantitative analysis. Natalie Eilam, Richard Hughes, Debbie Metcalf, and Diane Sanelli also contributed to the book's research. Chris Moos helped with references and the mechanics of the manuscript in its final stages.

Many colleagues reviewed drafts and gave valuable suggestions. Ted Rubin gave me the benefit of his broad knowledge about juvenile justice in the United States. Gary Corbett provided the perspective of one who has worked in many different roles in the juvenile justice system. Nancy Reichman asked hard questions that sent me back to make major revisions. Nancy Maron read the manuscript from the point of view of a state-level administrator and provided a balance for my local bias. Maggie Byrnes provided important insights into the problems of treating adolescents and the complex connection between funding and services. Kay Murray stimulated my thinking about the context of juvenile justice in large urban courts as well as in smaller courts. Barry Mahoney read the manuscript over and over again, in pieces and as a whole, and kept pushing me to think more critically and write more clearly. Our conversations often caused me to think about juvenile justice in new ways and helped me look at the court from a management perspective. Andrew Mandel provided invaluable assistance as editor of this book, as did Laura Skinger, the copyeditor. Editors Deborah Kops and Nancy Waring also played important roles in the book's earlier stages.

Dorene Miller typed much of the final version of the manuscript. She produced perfect copy in very short turnaround times on more occasions than either of us care to remember. She was preceded by another outstanding typist, Trudy Riedel, administrative assistant for the project. Jane Kristoffersen and Dawn Mayer also typed portions of the manuscript.

My family, Barry, Katie, and Michael Mahoney, supported me in innumerable ways through the writing of this book. They took over my share of household tasks when I was on writing binges, encouraged me when the project seemed without end, and celebrated with me when I finished segments.

The Juvenile Justice Network

Dreams and dollars establish the context for juvenile justice in the United States. Dreams tell us what justice for juveniles should be. Dollars pay for it. Both are generated in the community through a political process and channeled into the juvenile court. Both are constantly renegotiated between the community and the court and among agencies that work with the court.

A juvenile justice network, made up of the court and its related agencies, functions within a larger environment that is temporal, spatial, political, and economic. The network has a history, exists within a place, and negotiates with other organizations in the community to establish and maintain its ideologies and resources. The juvenile court's dream is a commitment to an optimistic view of human nature, a belief that behavior can be changed and that good intentions yield good results. As a society, we shaped that dream in 1899 into a special court for children. In 1967 the U.S. Supreme Court brought us to the realization that good intentions are not enough when it held in its landmark *Gault* decision that children, like adults, are entitled to due process of law.

With the *Gault* decision, the juvenile court, relatively stable since the turn of the century, entered a period of change that is still in progress. *Gault* precipitated revisions of state juvenile codes throughout the country, and Federal attention to delinquency spawned a series of "reforms"—experimental programs that brought new agencies and procedures into the court. Now after two decades of revamping and rethinking, the juvenile court is under attack and has no clear sense of direction. What is it doing? What is it supposed to do? How does it fit into a broader view of children's services and the legal system?

The purpose of this book is to explore the juvenile court's relations with its larger environment through an in-depth description of one court network, called here, "Suburban Court."[1] The book utilizes a social system framework that takes into account action within and between three organizational levels: the court's external environment, agencies within the court, and individual behavior. It is a story of myriad changes, shrinking resources, and shifting ideologies.

When we think about the court we tend to focus primarily on the court itself, on individual cases, on decision makers within it, and on its closely related agencies. Yet what goes on in the courtroom is influenced by a larger environment. An awareness of the contexual dimensions of the juvenile court is essential to an understanding of it and its decisions, and to the development and implementation of a coherent policy of justice for children.

The Juvenile Court as an Open System

Juvenile courts, like criminal courts, do not fit into traditional organizational models, which tend to emphasize authority from the top down, clearly specified organizational goals, and rational decision making. As Sarat (1977:4) notes, trial courts do not possess most of the characteristics that we commonly associate with complex organizations. They have no single structure of internal control or hierarchy and no central control of incentives or rewards (Eisenstein and Jacob, 1977; Mohr, 1976). Furthermore, courts theoretically do not create their own goals, but are dependent on the community for clarification of both goals and priorities. Yet courts *are* organizational, and we cannot understand the way they function or how they can change unless we take into account their peculiar organizational structure.

Two aspects are especially important. First is the court's dependence on its environment for ideologies, authority, clients, and resources (Bortner, 1982:225). This environment includes a variety of local, state, and federal funding units and the polities they represent, as well as child-serving agencies, families, and children.

The second aspect is that the "court" is not a single entity, but a network of related, yet autonomous organizations whose activities all revolve around a courtroom. The courtroom, with its presiding judge, is the symbolic center of the network where decisions are proclaimed and legitimated. Although it is useful to employ the terminology of the open systems model of structure to describe the court (as we will later), it is in fact less tightly connected than the word "system" implies; it is more like the organizational set described by Blau and Scott (1962), Evan (1966), or Weick (1976).

The social systems approach to organizations is useful for describing the implementation of change in organizations because it draws our attention to three levels of activity that form much of the organizations' context and directly and indirectly affect its decisions (Scheirer, 1981). The *macro level* focuses on decision making by legitimated organizational authorities, negotiations with other organizations, the acquisition and utilization of resources, and political, legal, and ideological pressures from the environment. The *intermediate or subunit level* addresses the internal processes of an organization or organizational network—factors such as role expectations of supervisors, standard operating rules and routines, communication flow, and work-group norms. These intermediate-level processes concern day-to-day work patterns that surround the introduction of new programs or policies and thus have an important impact on their success. The third level is the *individual level*, at which individual staff members promote or limit change to the extent that they understand it and are willing to modify their behavior to carry it out.

The open systems model allows us to think about organizations as connected in an interorganizational network (Benson, 1975) and decisions as collective products (Waegel, 1981). It focuses attention on the ways in which organizations strategically adapt to their environments (Aldrich and Pfeffer, 1976:3), engage in political interaction to retain or obtain control of real or symbolic resources (Bacharach and Lawler, 1980), and make internal decisions.[2]

The open systems model, then, provides a useful metaphor for our discussion of juvenile justice. It directs our attention to a court's dependence on its environment not only for resources, but also for legitimation, purpose, and clientele (Hasenfeld and Cheung, 1985). At the same time, it alerts us to the linkages among numerous small segments of an organization (Weick, 1985) and to an organization's need to continually renegotiate the conditions of its existence.

Suburban Court is like all courts in its ultimate economic and political dependence on its environment and the importance of its horizontal linkages. Variations in size, location, and organizational structure may influence outcomes of interactions between a court and its community, but the fact of a court's embeddedness in its environment is constant. No court is independent of its context, although we tend to study courts and court decisions as if they were.

By examining Suburban Court during a two-year period, I hope to illustrate the ways in which it and many other courts and their environments interact and to show how resource shifts, political in-fighting, personalities, experimental programs, and a changing political climate can shape a court and its decisions.

Dependence on the Environment

The juvenile justice network is dependent on its environment for ideologies, which give it its authority and clients, and for its resources. *Ideology* is defined here as it is used in recent sociological theories of organizations: It is a manner of thinking characteristic of a group or culture, a taken-for-granted normative system that can lend legitimacy to organizations and assert connections between an organization's assigned tasks and its chosen procedures (Benson, 1975:237; Meyer and Rowan, 1977).

Ideologies

Since its inception, the ideology of the juvenile court has developed as beliefs about children, offenders, and the legal system have shifted nationally and in local communities. The beliefs include assumptions about who children are, their relative importance, their needs, their appropriate behavior, and who is responsible for them. Beliefs about offenders include how they are defined, their relative importance, and how they should be treated. Beliefs about the legal system touch on issues of how justice is achieved and to whom it applies.

Changing Ideologies The juvenile court came into being in an era of strong reformist impulses. Over the years, however, federal, state, and local legislation has shifted its direction. The original paternalistic stance toward children that led to the development of informal hearings in 1899 has given way to a commitment to due process that has resulted in mini-criminal courts for chil-

dren. (Carey and McAnany, 1984:42; Fox, 1970; Hahn, 1984:168; Lemert, 5
1970). As a result of U.S. Supreme Court decisions in the 1960s and 1970s,
most states have revised their statutes regarding children and delinquency to
make courts more legalistic and their jurisdiction more specific (Levin and
Sarri, 1974).

Ambivalence about Ideologies   Juvenile courts are assigned the difficult task of
officially responding to youths who are alleged to be problems. Because most
communities are ambivalent about how delinquents should be handled, they
send the courts conflicting messages.

Society's message concerning its desire to act in the best interest of the
child may be mediated by other messages about law and order, community
safety, and cost efficiency. In principle, what is good for the child *should* be
good for society. In practice and over the short term, however, this may not
be obvious to all citizens and policy makers. For example, services for children,
especially delinquents, are costly, and in a world of finite resources, dollars
spent on juvenile justice are dollars taken away from other needy—and perhaps
more "deserving"—groups. Also, delinquents who are "given another chance"
or are released on legal technicalities may leave the court with an increased
respect for due process, or they may commit a more serious crime. An ongoing
tension remains between the best interests of the child and the best interests
of the community. Although this is in part what brought a specialized juvenile
court into existence in the first place, the court continually receives conflicting
messages.

Related to the issue of the best interest of the child is another dichotomy:
that of the two social statuses of child and offender. The child is viewed
traditionally as needing protection and nurturing. The offender is seen as
deserving punishment. Although this may oversimplify the highly complex
relationship among courts, communities, and juveniles who come before the
court, such ambivalence is very much a part of the response pattern and reflects
the ambivalence that many adults in our society feel toward adolescents. How
much of the community response toward juvenile offenders is prompted by
the youth's objective behavior and how much is motivated by a subjective
feeling of threat that adolescents pose to adults and to adult psychological,
organizational, and economic interests?

As a political economy, the court needs authority, sometimes called a
domain, which is the right and responsibility to carry out certain kinds of
programs (Benson, 1975: 229–232). Clients are part of a court's domain. Community ideology sets the guidelines for determining who enters the court
system, and provides gatekeepers, like police officers and child-care workers,

to determine who becomes a client. The court, as part of its domain, retains the right to reject certain kinds of clients, but beyond that can modify its population only by influencing the practices of its gatekeepers or by getting legislatures to change the laws.

Resources

We tend to think of courts as autonomous, but actually they operate under major constraints, especially since they do not generate income of their own and must rely on community resources. Many juvenile courts are part of state court systems where they almost invariably have low status. Indeed, the entire court system in some states is considered low status compared to other governmental units. Courts compete for resources and power like other organizations and often are at a disadvantage in the competition. In recent years, resources have flowed from all three levels of government: federal, state, and local. The community provides a variety of resources to the court, including money, facilities, time, and personnel. In the context of the juvenile court, this includes everything provided for children who enter the larger court network, from juvenile police units through diversion programs, court operations, and juvenile correctional facilities.

Resources can be expanded either by increasing them or by utilizing existing ones more effectively. Court delays may be reduced, for example, by adding judges or by making better use of a judge's time. The actual resource level is as important as the perceived level. Community A, with expanding resources, may view a given level of support positively because it is an increase over earlier levels. Community B, on the other hand, may view a similar level negatively because it represents either a decreased or static level in the face of growing needs.

Resources vs. Ideologies Ideologies and resources interact with society, one another, and the court itself to create a context within which a specific juvenile court operates and makes decisions about individual youths. The community has both dreams and dollars. Its dreams are goals born of its beliefs about children and community responsibility for them, about the potential that social institutions have to change lives, and about the importance of due process of law. Some dreams conflict, not surprisingly, since they emerge from the competing interests and alliances that make up American society.

Legislation, in theory but not always in practice, provides guidance about what the juvenile court is supposed to do, but community resource allocations often give other messages about the real priorities. (Programs are sometimes mandated, for example, without funds being allocated.) The court is expected to protect the child and the community and to act on adolescent offenders without forsaking the best interest of the individual child—all within a limited budget. The real price of services is frequently hard to track, given the intricacies of federal, state, and local cost-sharing arrangements. As a result, court workers who are concerned about resource constraints may have little solid information about actual costs or where reductions might be made to least compromise court goals. When priorities are unclear, it is hard to use existing resources well. They tend to be wasted in nonproductive ways—excessive paperwork, meetings that go nowhere concerning issues that no one can do anything about, hearings that can't be held because someone or something is missing, agencies that have no real function. It is hard to make decisions without clear priorities about how to use resources.

Shrinking Resources   Funds for human services, including those for children, suffered cutbacks in the early 1980s. As resources diminish or are reallocated in response to changing definitions of societal needs, courts and children's services compete for limited resources and have to make a strong case for why they need them. These sharp resource reductions may be reversed somewhat, but they probably harbinger a new reality for the financing of all human services. As Lawson and Gletne (1982:45) warn, limitation of resources for courts is a virtual certainty, and it stems not only from a particular set of political actions, but also from a larger understanding that money, like natural resources, is not without limit.

The traditional juvenile court movement, emphasizing the best interest of the child as its first priority, made the implicit assumption that whatever money was necessary should be available for court services. Advocates of the juvenile court movement have argued that if the movement has failed, it is because it was never given adequate resources (Krisberg and Austin, 1978:568; White House Conference on Child Health and Protection, 1932). Yet services for juveniles proliferated in the 1960s and 1970s (Galvin and Polk, 1983:325), while solutions to the delinquency problem, at either an individual or societal level, seemed no closer. The "more money, more services" approach did not solve the juvenile delinquency problem.

It is unclear whether the court's continuing failure to meet early expectations results from lack of resources or their inappropriate use, lack of knowledge or just mistaken premises about what is possible. What is clear, however, is that resources for the court in the future are going to be less plentiful than they have been in the recent past, in part because advocates of the "more, more, more" approach did not make a good case for it when resources were at their peak. Particularly in the next decade, with age distribution tipping toward the over 65 group and the proportion of the population under 18 dropping, children's services in general may be seen by policy makers as a lower priority.[3] A juvenile justice system built on a model of spiraling needs and costs, as the present system seems to have been, may have difficult times ahead. Negotiations between the court network and the community may become increasingly fierce as the court endeavors to continue to expand, or at least *maintain* its level of community support.

Time as a Resource   Time is a resource of particular importance for the juvenile court, since its jurisdiction is, by nature, limited to a narrow band in an individual's life (roughly from age 10 to 17). Time can be bought with other resources, like additional judges, increased staff, and more courtrooms, or it can be extended, within limits, by more efficient use. As a court's environment changes, its need and use of time shifts. Theoretically, changes can result in a need for less time, but more often courts experience expanding demands on their time in conjunction with constant or declining resources.

A substantial body of literature has been developed on case processing time (e.g., Church, et al. 1978a; Mahoney, Sipes, and Ito 1985), but until recently there has been limited attention to time use in juvenile courts. At present groups such as the Institute of Judicial Administration and American Bar Association (IJA-ABA) Juvenile Justice Standards Committee (1980a), the National Conference of State Trial Judges (1984), and the Conference of State Court Administrators (1983), along with some state legislatures (e.g., Florida in its 1981 revision of its Rule of Juvenile Procedure) are developing time standards and speedy trial rules for juveniles. These standards put further resource pressure on juvenile courts that want to operate within recommended time frames but cannot without increasing personnel or making better use of available time.

The Problem of Change Overload

The juvenile justice system's dependence on the larger community leaves it vulnerable to changes within that community, as well as within its own domain. Change may come from external events, such as new legislation and revised funding levels, or from internal factors, like personnel turnover or agency restructuring.

Organizations and individuals cope with potential and actual changes in a variety of ways. Initially they may try to influence the direction of change to make it as compatible as possible with their original objectives. This may be difficult, however, if they cannot agree on goals and priorities. Once a change is mandated for the court, participants may accept it or try to neutralize its impact through narrow interpretation or informal redefinition. Some participants may even try to turn changes, or the resultant confusion, to their own organizational advantage.

Change is a constant in many juvenile courts as legislators and policy makers continually tinker with codes and treatment programs while new agencies and the shuffling of agency responsibilities keep organizational relationships continually in flux. One reason change continues in this fashion is that the court's role remains undefined. It should operate within a network of services for children, but because we are unsure about how we want to treat young people and what priority to place on their needs, we don't give the court clear signals. Without such a consensus the court is vulnerable to the community's current attitudes about children. New programs rise and fall; resources are prey to fads of theory and policy. Rapid change can put a heavy burden of continual adaptation on a court. The overload it produces is akin to the overload Walker (1981) describes in intergovernmental relations. The more the environment is in flux, the more problematic it becomes for the court system and the more concerned court agencies may be about finalizing agreements with the community regarding their objectives and procedures.

Reforms, if they are to produce any significant impact on a system, must disrupt the system's balance sufficiently to induce participants to engage in new behavior. A reform, as used here, refers to a statement of a policy preference that contradicts operations and priorities reflected in current practice (Nimmer, 1978:175). As a result, it generates disagreement as well as readjustment within the system. The disagreement may become especially acute when a reform is mandated without allocation of sufficient funds, necessitating shifts in priorities and resource use.

Internal change at the intermediate level has accelerated in the court as the number of agencies involved in its work proliferate. New interest groups, agencies, and individuals, all with particular ideologies and economic interests, move in and out of the juvenile justice system. The introduction of defense attorneys into juvenile courts, for example, upset their internal balance as lawyers trained in the adversarial techniques of trial practice tried to establish their role in a court lacking opposing counsel. Judges consequently found themselves pushed into the role of state's attorney and soon jurisdictions were rewriting their codes to include state's attorneys or prosecutors.

In many jurisdictions the juvenile court is one of several courts through which newly hired prosecutors and public defenders rotate. New attorneys advancing through the court hierarchy often try to stay as briefly as possible in the low-status juvenile court, and their rapid turnover keeps the court in a constant state of adaptation. The small work group in the courtroom is a delicately balanced unit, bound together by shared expectations (Mileski, 1971); a new person who does not know or adhere to that set of expectations can throw the whole unit off.

Literature concerning the impact on courts of specific legislative or procedural changes (e.g., Sarri and Hasenfeld, 1976; Stapleton and Teitlebaum, 1972; Wasby, 1970), rarely takes into account the impact of constant change. Again, this kind of change frequently costs individuals and agencies time and energy. These costs are difficult to measure, but the hours devoted to adjusting to such changes—new personnel, new procedures, new alliances between agencies and individuals—are hours taken away from direct service to clients. Ideally, the changes are positive and improve services so that initial adjustment cost is recouped as service gets better. But change does not always yield better service, even when supported by adequate resources. As Empey notes (1980:157), "At the very least, one should be cautious about equating change with progress."

Change can also increase the number of decisions made by individuals and organizations at macro, intermediate, and individual levels of activity since it renders problematic activities and procedures that had previously been routinized and requires new efforts at coordination. The more decisions there are, the more coordination becomes necessary, and the higher the communication load (Farace, Monge, and Russell, 1977:104). When either individuals or systems reach a point where they cannot process incoming communication as rapidly as they would like to, an overload results. Overload, for an individual or a system, is generally associated with stress. Communication research shows that as demands for coordination and action reach capacity, increases in input fail to result in any further increases in output. The person or system goes into what communication experts call a "confusional state," and output starts to drop. If the input rate continues to climb, output rates continue to decline (Farace, Monge, and Russell, 1977: 108, 110–111).

Much of the juvenile court's work in achieving its goals involves communication and coordination. It is possible that many courts run close to communication capacity most of the time. We can speculate that constant change can move an already heavily loaded system like the juvenile court into periodic or chronic states of overload as individuals and agencies continually work to adapt to new rules and forge new personal and organizational liaisons. New programs, new people, and new codes keep the system in constant flux.

There are few baselines against which to measure achievement, and participants who are overworked and overwhelmed may find fewer rewards in their work.

Change in itself is not bad. The ability to change is essential to an organization's adaptation to its environment and ultimate ability to survive. But change carries time and energy costs. Constant change, without any clear direction or underlying philosophy, can drain an organization of its creative energy.

Network of Agencies, Variety of Dreams

A network is a group of autonomous organizations that interact with each other yet have other activities and concerns. It can be conceived of as a political economy concerned with the distribution of two scarce resources—money and authority (Benson, 1975: 229).

Units of the court network—linked agencies, governmental units, and individuals—may theoretically share the goals and ideologies of the court, which is the symbolic center of the network, the arena in which players attempt to resolve their own and the community's conflicts over how to handle people accused of wrongdoing. Politically, economically, and organizationally, however, this is an unrealistic assumption. Agencies can agree on matters of domain and ideology only to the extent that such agreement does not threaten their interests. There is a problem when domain claims of two agencies are in conflict, or when each claims the same or similar sphere of activity (Benson, 1975: 237).

Just as the court competes with other units in its environment for resources and control, so do agencies and occupational groups in the court network compete with each other at the intermediate level. Each has its own goals, and is responding to the impact of decreasing resources. To justify their share of available resources—and perhaps even their existence—individuals, as representatives of their agencies, need to prove that they attract clients and are successful, i.e., that they meet needs in the network. As Drabek and Chapman (1973:362) note, much of organizational life is a reflection of bargaining behavior. Organizational incumbents seek to renegotiate constraining expectations others have of them so they can maintain and expand their "existing levels of autonomy, security, and prestige." Agencies must ultimately develop either a carefully worked out compromise in which the interests of all relevant agencies are protected or a solution in which one agency's interests are upheld at the expense of others.

The open systems model recognizes the normality and reality of conflict between formal system goals and the goals of individual and organizational players within the organization. At the same time, it draws attention to the system of controls, incentives, and sanctions at the system's disposal (Feeley, 1973:414).

Often, however, networks do not manifest clear-cut dominance patterns in which one or a few organizations are all-powerful. Frequently, several parties confront each other on nearly equal terms. These kinds of networks are often blocked or noncooperative because all agencies suffer from resource shortages and none can master enough power to dictate terms to others (Benson, 1975:234–35). A court in which this situation exists may get ambiguous messages about how it should handle delinquency and may find decision making difficult (Hannan and Freeman, 1977:930; Scott, 1981:116).

The multiple objectives of the court and the variety of agencies within its network also have important implications for its functioning. In decision making, multiple objectives need to be assigned priorities. If the goal structure does not provide an adequate basis for selecting among alternatives, i.e., if goals are vaguely defined, unranked, or posed in terms which make operational implementation difficult, individuals and groups can press their personal and unit goals regardless of the impact on the larger organizational environment (Jones, 1982:7). Under these conditions, organizational subunits will tend to promote their own self-interests unless constrained or otherwise directed, and will propose decisions and programs that will concentrate on furthering their own welfare (Jones, 1982:8).

A pervasive theme running through this book involves ongoing community ambivalence about troublesome children and the impact of this ambivalence upon the goals and procedures of juvenile courts. Figure 1.1 illustrates this interaction between courts and communities. As the next chapter documents, from the early days of the juvenile court there has been confusion about the nature of children's rights. Should children in the juvenile court be viewed as children or offenders? Are they entitled primarily to nurturance or due process of law? Which takes precedence—the best interest of the child or the best interest of the community? A second major concern is the procedure for implementing children's rights. Which representative of the community is responsible for protecting the rights of children? Who is accountable for the treatment of the community's troubled children?

Because the community is unclear about its responsibility to children, it fails to send clear messages to the court about appropriate objectives and procedures. The court attempts to resolve the ambiguities through negotiation at all levels of the court network. This process may yield variation in decisions

Figure
I.I
The interaction between communities and juvenile courts
13

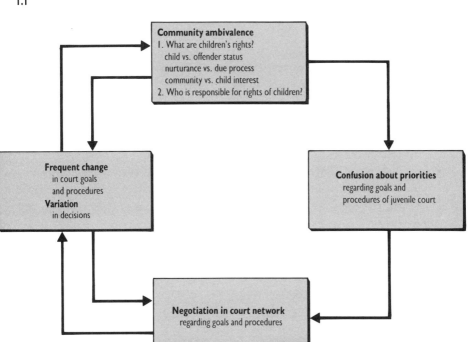

across jurisdictions as different networks reach different resolutions of the issues. It may also result in frequent, sometimes extreme, shifts in court goals and procedures, especially when ambivalence and dissatisfaction about courts are high in the community. These changes and variations reverberate back to the court network, often prompting a new round of negotiations that in turn may yield more change and more variations. They also may affect community attitudes, reinforcing ambivalence or a feeling of the need for change.

The fabric of the juvenile justice system, the success of its reforms, and the range of decision options available to it depend upon the outcomes of the network's internal and external negotiations. We have tended in the past to focus much of our research on the courts' responses to individual cases. The emphasis in this book is on the complex organizational interactions that yield the range of dispositional options available to a court when it responds to an individual child. Our primary focus is on the negotiations within the court network regarding goals and procedures.

The negotiations described here took place in Suburban Court from January 1, 1980 through June 30, 1982. Our study involved the collection of both observational and court record data. Records were examined and coded for all youths who had a delinquency petition filed in the court during 1980 (710) and also for those who were sent by the District Attorney to the District Attorney's Diversion Project (452). The unit of analysis is the *youth* rather than the *case*, and cases involving the same youth were consolidated during data collection. An extensive code was used to collect data on legal variables, case processing times, and family information. Pending cases were followed up in late August, 1981, eight months after the end of the data collection period, in order to maximize the number of completed cases. Cases still pending then were coded as such with a written explanation of the case's circumstances and future dates for appearance.

Qualitative data included observation notes culled from a year of daily observation of delinquency cases in 1980; notes from participant observers in three court agencies; observations of all regular meetings of an interagency policy-making group; formal and informal interviews with judges, lawyers, and agency staff members; newspaper clippings; and a variety of agency memos and reports.

The research staff worked full time in the Suburban Court and its agencies for over a year, with some preliminary involvement before the project started and a continuing presence for a year and a half after the primary observational period ended. Throughout the book, references to observational, interview, or agency materials are identified as Suburban Youth Project (SYP) followed by a page number. Appendix A describes in detail the researchers' efforts to fit themselves into the court as well as the detailed coding instructions that were used for the court records.

Involvement with the different agencies of the court and its environment and direct observation of the court in progress provided insight into the different dimensions of the court's context, as well as into its daily operations and decisions. For the most part, Suburban Court has had a reputation from its earliest days as a "good court," committed to fairness and due process and staffed by caring, concerned, and skilled personnel. It operates under a Children's Code that is generally considered to be well framed and oriented toward the protection of children's rights.

The court can be classified in the multidimensional typology developed by Stapleton, Aday, and Ito (1982) as a Type IV Autonomous/Interventionist court, their second most frequent type of court. Its rules of adjudication are those commonly associated with the notion of due process. State intervention is predicated on the conduct, not the condition of the child; there is prescreening by the prosecutor, fact finding is based on adversary process, and decision making is limited by rules and structure.

The Type IV court is an association of work groups who share a common ideology, but whose day-to-day activities are structured and organized by their participation in different "sponsoring" organizations. These work groups participate in a case, but they are bound more by loose interorganizational ties than by an integrated bureaucratic structure headed by a judge. The judge is dominant in the courtroom, but his or her authority is limited outside that setting in that the judiciary is neither the primary employer nor the exclusive organizer of the other related work groups (Stapleton, Aday, and Ito, 1982).

For a variety of reasons—new state legislation, federal demonstration programs, local financial problems—Suburban Court was, at the time of our study, in the process of renegotiating its role. Like other juvenile courts throughout the country, it struggled in the 1970s and early 1980s with growing case loads, changing legal requirements, and shifting budget priorities. In describing the negotiations over dreams and resources within Suburban Court and between the court and its environment, my goal is to increase understanding about the ways in which societal institutions interact to yield policies and decisions that affect individual citizens. The particular institution described in this case is the juvenile court, but the negotiations of that court and its environment are instructive concerning the nature of negotiations in other institutions and environments.

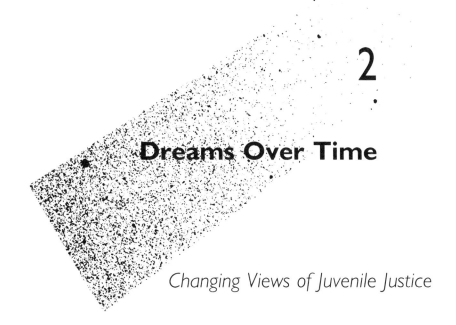

2

Dreams Over Time

Changing Views of Juvenile Justice

The history of the American juvenile justice system is an integral part of our nation's political, social, and intellectual history. Early advocates of special courts for children were strongly influenced by the ideology of the progressive movement, and especially by its optimism about the ability to effect positive change in individuals and the social system. Through half a century of sweeping social change, the court has grappled with a difficult set of issues, many of which remain unresolved today. What rights do children have, and how do we define them? Whom do we charge with the responsibility for our children, and how do we hold them accountable? How much discretion is necessary, or desirable?

Attempts to resolve these issues have shaped the ongoing negotiations about ideologies among child advocates and other members of the community. Figure 2.1 summarizes the history of the juvenile court as it moved from the efforts of early reformers to develop separate facilities for juveniles in the late 1800s to the U.S. Supreme Court decisions and national legislative initiatives regarding juvenile courts in the 1960s and 1970s.

Figure 2.1   **Context over time: changing ideologies and the juvenile court**

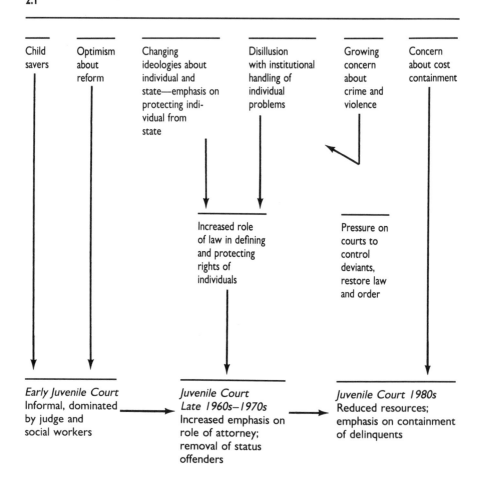

Early Reformers—One Version of Best Interest

The early "child saving movement," as Platt (1969:75) calls it, developed in the mid-1890s primarily through the efforts of feminist reformers in Chicago, who had organized earlier attempts to provide separate houses of refuge for children in New York, Philadelphia, Boston, and Chicago (Mennel, 1973; Platt, 1969). Their work culminated in 1899, when the Illinois legislation created in Cook County, Chicago, the first juvenile court through an act entitled "A Law for the Care of Dependent, Neglected, and Delinquent Chil- dren." The statute provided for a specialized court with a specialized law relating to children, restricted the jailing of children under twelve years of age, allowed for the appointment of probation officers and stated a legislative purpose to reform rather than punish (Rubin, 1984).

Sutton (1985:108–110) argues that there was nothing new and distinctive about the juvenile court, that it was primarily a ceremonial institution through which the ideology of the charity organization movement was enacted, and that it was a way for the legal system to appear responsive to demands for individualized therapeutic justice without altering its decision-making routines. Nevertheless, the juvenile court concept continued to expand, and strong support for special handling of juveniles was guaranteed by the rapid adoption of juvenile court legislation. By 1917, such legislation had been passed in all but three states, and by 1932 there were over 600 independent juvenile courts in the United States (Platt, 1969:10).

Judge Ben Lindsey (1904), an active and enthusiastic promoter of special courts for children, gives a sense of the ideology of early juvenile courts in his description of his own court in Denver, Colorado:

> The whole proceeding is in the interest of the child and not to degrade him or even to punish him. We do not protect the child by discharging him because there is no legal evidence to convict, as would be done in a criminal case when we know that he has committed the offense. This is to do him a great injury . . .

As illustrated above, the early court advocates proceeded with a clear sense of what children needed. They believed, for example, that children could be saved from a life of crime if they were properly disciplined and protected from bad influences. The movement took the public school, and not the family, as its model and assumed that the interests of children could best be served through a regimen of education, hard work, and strict discipline (Empey, 1982).

Recent historians (Fox, 1970; Platt, 1969) argue that a middle class fear of the "dangerous classes" and the desire to control them was an important influence on early reformers and that their motivations were not so much benign as controlling. Many of the children placed in houses of refuge were the offspring of immigrants, and one historian (Schlossman, 1977:24) notes that an early reformer described the house of refuge as ". . . an instrument for compelling lower class children to conform to middle class standards of behavior." He argues that the reformers' view of the best interest of the child reflected both middle-class values and a middle-class need to protect its life-style.

This view, which was given strong credence by Platt's book, *The Child Savers* (1969), has become widely accepted over the past several years. It is ideologically compatible with the present trend toward limitation of discretion and the development of a more legalistic juvenile court. The view is not, however, held unanimously (Conrad, 1981:179). J. Lawrence Schultz, for example, argues that it was not just the middle class who sought court control of immigrant youths. Immigrant parents often actively sought the court's assistance with their unruly offspring, and early judges often characterized their most difficult cases as those in which parents wanted the court to rid them of their children. In fact, it was often the probation officers who saved children from the reformatory when parents urged the court to send them away (Schultz, 1973). Thus, community treatment under the supervision of a probation officer became the philosophical ideal (Empey, 1980:159–163).

The beliefs and aspirations that led to the creation of the juvenile court are best understood as a kind of visionary theorizing about children and the best way to nurture and protect them (Empey, 1980). These beliefs emerged from a positivistic school of thought that focused on the individual rather than the offense, and stressed the importance of an individual's environment rather than his or her free will. Deviant children were viewed as victims rather than offenders (Fox, 1970). From this perspective, early promoters of the court believed that it could rescue children and become a benevolent surrogate for ineffective families. They believed that the court could *prevent* delinquency by identifying the "first conditions of neglect or delinquency" and intervening in the child's life before the child became "criminal in tastes and habits" (Platt, 1969:138–139). In other words, child advocates saw the juvenile court as a means of decriminalizing and rehabilitating children, rather than punishing them.

The high hopes of the early proponents of the juvenile court are described poignantly by Robert Hutchins in 1976 in his foreword to *Pursuing Justice for the Child*:

> When I graduated from law school some fifty years ago, the aspiring liberals among us thought we knew what was the trouble with the law. It was too narrow and too formalistic . . . The juvenile court, then only twenty-five years old, reflected the responsibility of the state as *parens patriae*, which could rescue children from the law, and from those agents of government whom we did not trust, like policemen, prosecutors, judges in criminal courts, and wardens of jails and penitentiaries. It could even rescue children from their parents. To us the juvenile court, with

which few of us had any experience, looked like the fulfillment of our
dreams . . .

Hutchins's reminiscence reflects beliefs about children's rights, including rights to life, food, clothing, shelter, and proper moral standards to follow that came from a concept of English law under which the King of England protected the property interests of fatherless children. Known as *parens patriae* ("parent of the nation"), this doctrine was adapted by the court to authorize the juvenile court judges to intervene in the lives of children as they saw fit.

Rules covering dependent and neglected children were similar to those covering delinquent children. In most states, children accused of truancy and being unmanageable were not differentiated from children who committed crimes. These children are known as *status offenders* because they come to the attention of the court by virtue of their status as children allegedly involved in behavior not prohibited for adults but thought undesirable for children.

Children who came into the court, for whatever reason, were assumed to be dependent persons, and the principles of due process did not apply to them (Empey, 1982). It is important to remember that although early architects of the juvenile court were concerned about children's rights, they were concerned about nurturance rights rather than due process rights. Court founders battled for improved child labor laws, racial equality, and educational, vocational, and recreational opportunities for all children (Polier, 1974:113). They saw these issues as more important than due process rights.

Child vs. Offender

A delinquent child has two statuses: that of *child* and that of *offender*. This dual status yields a dichotomous response from a community that wants to protect its children but be protected from its offenders. Children need to be helped, guided, and nurtured; offenders defy community values, can be dangerous, and need to be punished.

Emphasis in the early court was very much, perhaps too much, on the delinquent's status as *child*. The juvenile court of 1899 attempted to balance justice and security and to communicate the greater importance of the child status over the offender status through its rehabilitative ideal and in its procedures. Such efforts, however, were not always successful. Although the climate of public opinion was supportive of a positivistic approach to juvenile offenders (Shichor, 1983), the community also stressed security. Courts, despite informal and closed proceedings and continually changing euphemisms for crime, criminals, guilt, and prison, could not protect children from the stigmatization of court involvement. As communities came increasingly to believe that the "children" were committing a growing percentage of serious and violent crimes, the courts found it harder to treat delinquents as helpless children needing guidance (McNally, 1983:32; Nejelski, 1977).

Early courts essentially denied the existence of adolescence and today's court terminology still reflects that attitude. An adolescent is referred to as "the minor child who committed an act which if committed by an adult would be a crime." A judge tells a six-foot fifteen-year-old to go home and mind his mother. The treatment of young adults as children denies part of their normal struggle to become functioning adults. It also makes the court appear naive to community members who are afraid of the young men and women who rob and assault them.

Community Interest vs. Child Interest

The underlying assumption that the child's interest and the community's interest are the same has created tension throughout the history of the juvenile court. As Allen notes (1964:51), these interests may not be equatable. The juvenile court is legally mandated to act in the "best interests of the child," but it also is expected by the taxpayers who finance it to protect them from victimization by either removing dangerous youths from the community or reforming them. Pound observed in 1944 (pp. 2–4) that general security has been the most obvious social interest and the one most pressed by the community. Allen speculates that the early court, in failing to recognize this community protection function, blinded itself to the structural limitations of its role and, as a consequence, set itself up for conflict with the community (1964: 50).

In a chapter entitled, "The Juvenile Court and the Limits of Juvenile Justice" from *The Borderland of Criminal Justice*, Allen articulated many of the issues that had been bubbling beneath the surface of the juvenile court. He suggested that the community's tendency to attribute capabilities to the court that it does not possess (e.g., delinquency prevention and treatment) represents an unpremeditated effort to evade accepting more fundamental and less comfortable solutions to handling child offenders (1964:60).

Discretion—The Two-Edged Sword

A decision maker has discretion whenever "the effective limits of his power leave him free to make a choice among possible causes of action or inaction" (Davis, 1969:4). Early framers of the juvenile court recognized the importance and necessity of discretion and built the juvenile court upon it. Juvenile court judges need discretion in order to administer individualized justice. It is essential to full consideration of children's unique circumstances and determination of their "best interests." The ideal envisions justice as a personal experience. Bortner (1982:8) describes a transcendent justice "not confined to the average or established, but a superior justice finely tuned to restore harmony between the individual and the collective."

We both need and fear discretion. It is an important safety valve in a complex system, a means of fending off bureaucratic authority and individualizing solutions to problems. Yet it can also be used to subvert both the regulations and intent of institutions, and to promote the well-being of some citizens, usually those with power, at the expense of others, usually those without power. As Katkin (1980) notes, ". . . a law without discretion cannot exist . . . the practical problem is entirely a matter of dosage. How much discretion ought there to be?"

Feeley (1973:420) identifies two components in the problem of discretion: the sheer magnitude of substantive laws and procedural rules, and the inherent ambiguity of these rules. Since it is not possible to enforce all rules, there must be room to select which will be administered. Ambiguity allows leeway in several areas, including the process of selecting which facts to consider and which rules to apply. Ambiguity allows latitude for discretion and for bargaining, but also enables rules to be used as "weapons or supports at the whim of, or in the particular interests of, the various actors in the system." Herbert Packer (1968:290) notes, "The basic trouble with discretion is simply that it is *lawless*, in the literal sense of that term."

Early reformers of juvenile court were not unduly concerned about the "lawless dimension" of discretion.[1] Caught up in the optimism of the era and convinced of the strength of professionalism, they trusted that judges would use it wisely. As experience with the juvenile courts accumulated, however, thoughtful observers in courts, corrections, and educational institutions began to express growing concern about it (Sprowls, 1980).

By the 1960s the social climate in the United States was heavy with distrust of both government and discretion. Civil rights activists pointed to ways in which discretionary power allowed decision makers to discriminate against minority groups and women. Proponents of labeling theory implied that the negative stigma of formal processing of juveniles was often differentially applied to youths according to class or ethnic status, and could actually promote further delinquent behavior by labeled youths (Schur, 1973). One of the areas in which discretion and its accompanying differential labeling was most decried was in juvenile court.

Lawyers and civil libertarians argued that treatment of juvenile offenders often involved punishment as severe as that meted out to adults, and that children, like adults, should not have their liberty taken away without due process of law (Allen, 1964). Bortner (1982:8–9) maintains that the implementation of the ideal of discretion may be so impeded within the present social context of the juvenile court that it provides a cloak for discrimination rather than individualized justice.

Organizational expediency, structural inequalities, professional ideologies, and the idiosyncracies of decision makers all may take precedence over individual juvenile needs.

Dissatisfaction Grows

Given the unresolved issues plaguing juvenile courts in the mid-20th century, it is not surprising that optimism about the court began to fade. What is surprising is that the juvenile court was allowed to go for so long—over half a century—without serious inquiry into its accomplishments. It was clear relatively early to observers and those who worked in the court that it had not met the high expectations surrounding its inception.

Not only did the court fail to resolve the difficulties of troubled and troublesome children but it also created some new problems. As early as 1937 Roscoe Pound, a supporter of the juvenile court, referred to it as "a tribunal more awesome in its abuse of power than the star chamber" (Pound, 1937: xxxviii). In 1947, Paul Tappan, a strong advocate for due process, stated that neither society's present state of knowledge nor the court's record justified the court's preventive intervention in the lives of children.

Dissatisfaction with the court continued to rise. Criticisms of the court reflected a growing concern about the rights of juveniles, including a distrust of discretion, the awareness of potential stigmatization of court appearance, and an increased appreciation of individual rights (Ketcham, 1961). It also reflected opposition from the other direction: Violence was rising in American cities and fear of crime was on the upturn. Citizens concerned about spiraling delinquency rates, the weakening of the family and traditional American values, and growing violence nationwide questioned the effectiveness of the court to contain juvenile misbehavior. Community ambivalence yielded what Herbert Packer (1968) described as two differing models for the juvenile courts: the "due process model"—or adherence to legal rules and an adversary relationship—and the "crime control model"—which stresses protection of the community and minimizes formality and individual rights. Citizens also railed against the court's secrecy and judicial discretion, which could release a youth back into the community almost before the arresting police officer returned to work. By the 1960s concern had reached serious proportions. Early in his presidency, John F. Kennedy appointed the President's Committee on Juvenile Delinquency and Youth Crime, chaired by his brother, Attorney General Robert Kennedy. After Kennedy's assassination, Lyndon B. Johnson appointed a new Commission on Law Enforcement and Administration of Justice, whose proceedings and recommendations (which came to be known as the President's Commission Report) were published in 1967, the same year that the influential *Gault* decision was handed down by the U.S. Supreme Court. The Report cited problems in the juvenile court, particularly the stigma of the delinquency label and ineffective services (Fabricant, 1983).

In the report, Edwin Lemert charged that the court's later years had been a period of "unmet promise and darkened with growing controversy." Evidence that a juvenile court prevents crime or decreases recidivism is missing, he claimed, and it may actually contribute to juvenile crime by imposing on children stigma, unwise detention, and incarceration in institutions that corrupt rather than reform (1967:91). The report was highly influential, and it was cited nine times in the important *Gault* Supreme Court case that came shortly after (Horowitz, 1977:176).

The Supreme Court's Role in Shaping Juvenile Justice

In the mid 1960s amidst a general concern about civil rights, expanded rights for adult criminal defendants, and the growing dissatisfaction with the juvenile court (Rubin, 1984:93), lawyers and advocates for children's rights began to look more closely at the juvenile court and identify cases that were cause for concern. Within a period of ten years, the Supreme Court would hand down five major decisions that significantly affected the structure of American juvenile justice. The most far-reaching of these was *In re Gault* in 1967.

In re Gault is the case of a fifteen-year-old boy sentenced to six years' incarceration for making obscene phone calls, an offense that would have resulted in a maximum imprisonment of 60 days for an adult. The potential for abuse of discretion in the secretive and informal juvenile court became apparent in the Supreme Court transcripts, and after reading them, one's faith in the old dreams of the early juvenile court can never be as strong.

Gault held that a child not only has the right to a lawyer and to a free lawyer if indigent, but also that written notice of the specifics of the offense must be provided for children and parents, that children have the right to cross-examine witnesses against them, and that children are protected against self-incrimination.

Four other decisions also signaled the Supreme Court's determination to mold and monitor actions in juvenile courts.

Kent v. U.S. (1966) asserted that in procedures concerning transfer from juvenile court to criminal court, due process fairness must attach. Justice Fortas summarized the rising dissatisfaction with juvenile court: ". . . there may be grounds for concern that the child receives the worst of both worlds: that he gets neither the protections accorded to adults nor the solicitous care and regenerative treatment postulated for children" (383 U.S. at 555).

In re Winship (1970) ruled that the measure of proof in the trial of a juvenile charged with an act that would constitute a crime if committed by an adult must be beyond a reasonable doubt—the same standard used in adult criminal cases.

McKeiver v. Pennsylvania (1971) reverted to an earlier rationale in ruling that the federal constitution did not compel states to provide the right of jury trial to an accused juvenile. A state could, however, legislate this option, or its appellate court could determine that its state constitution required the right to jury trial for juveniles within the state. As of 1974, eleven states had allowed jury trials for children charged with delinquency, either by statute or by case decision (Levin and Sarri, 1974).

Breed v. Jones (1975) ruled that the double jeopardy clause of the Fifth Amendment applies, through the Fourteenth Amendment, to juveniles. This decision prevented a juvenile from being adjudicated in the juvenile court and then transferred to an adult court where a harsher sentence could be imposed. This created an important constitutional protection, since earlier cases had held that the double jeopardy prohibition did not prevent subsequent conviction in criminal court or successive juvenile proceedings arising out of the same conduct, because juvenile proceedings were civil and protective, and not criminal and punitive (Wadlington, Whitebread, and Davis, 1983:252).

Taken together, these five decisions assured that juvenile proceedings would be carried on in a court of law rather than at an informal hearing, and its procedures would be regularized in accordance with constitutional requirements. The decisions also played an important role in questioning the limits of official discretion. These and other legislation of the late 1960s and early 1970s were all aimed at narrowing the discretion that had been put in the hands of juvenile judges and probation officers (Sprowls, 1980).

The Supreme Court decisions left unanswered, however, some key questions regarding juvenile justice. For example, a fundamental ambiguity is identified by Schultz and Cohen (1976:25): Is a delinquency proceeding an analogue to a criminal proceeding in substance and procedure, or is it a search to identify a condition requiring treatment or rehabilitation? In other words, the question once again is whether the delinquent is essentially a child or an 27 offender.

Fox (1970) raised a related question about whether child welfare responsibilities—the nurturance rights taken on by the state as part of the original juvenile court commitment to children—could be rescinded as due process rights were reinstituted to children. In the 1899 court, juveniles had, in essence, been promised humane kindness in return for their constitutional rights. As those rights were reinstated, did states come to see themselves as relieved of their obligation to provide resources for nurturance?

Although the Gault decision moved the court toward a due process model and a more formalized procedure, it is debatable whether it added substantially to community protection. To many community observers, it was a move in the opposite direction, as deliquents won dismissals on legal technicalities and bargained for reduced charges. There arose what Ohlin (1983:466) describes as a "strong conservative reaction to the liberal policies advocated by crime commissions." Adherents of both the due process model and the crime control model continued to be concerned about discretion in the court (Packer, 1968).

Executive and Legislative Attention to Juvenile Justice

Trends that brought juvenile courts to the attention of Appellate Courts were also focusing executive and legislative attention on juvenile offenders.

The President's Commission Report in 1967 recommended reforms that fell under four headings that have come to be known as the 4D's: decriminalization, diversion, due process, and deinstitutionalization. *Decriminalization* centered in particular on the removal of status offenders from the jurisdiction of the juvenile court. *Diversion* involved the channeling of first-time and petty offenders away from legal processing and into community institutions. *Due process*, was given special support by the Supreme Court's *Gault* decision, moved the juvenile court closer to the model of adult criminal courts by mandating the involvement of attorneys in juvenile cases. *Deinstitutionalization* stressed the importance of developing correctional programs that utilized open community settings whenever possible, as an alternative to isolated, locked institutions (Empey, 1978:532–533) The recommendations triggered both national and state legislative efforts on behalf of juveniles.

Within a year, Congress passed the Juvenile Delinquency Prevention and Control Act of 1968, which was to be administered by the Youth Development and Delinquency Prevention Administration (YDDPA) of the Department of Health, Education, and Welfare. There was some dissatisfaction with HEW's implementation of the act, however, and because of Congressional pressure, federal agencies in 1971 agreed that the YDDPA would concentrate its efforts on programs outside of the juvenile justice system, including Youth Service Bureaus. The Law Enforcement Assistance Administration, then a new agency within the Department of Justice, would focus on the juvenile justice system itself through an agreement embodied in more new legislation, called the Juvenile Delinquency Prevention Act of 1972 (LEAA Legislative History, 1974).

Concern about crime continued to have high political salience, leading the Nixon administration to set up another national commission in 1973—the National Advisory Commission on Criminal Justice Standards and Goals. It, too, recommended decriminalization, deinstitutionalization, due process, and diversion (National Advisory Commission, 1976). These recommendations, in turn, were reflected in additional legislation involving juveniles—the Juvenile Justice and Delinquency Prevention Act of 1974. The 1974 Act phased out the youth services of YDDPA and created a new office, the Office of Juvenile Justice and Delinquency Prevention, whose intent was to promote the 4D's. Significantly, it was located in LEAA—not HEW—a shift from the welfare realm to the justice realm of the government.

The JJDP Act of 1974 stipulated that to be eligible for federal funding for state juvenile delinquency programs, states had two years in which to plan for (1) the removal of status offenders from locked pre-trial detention centers, and (2) the end of commitment of status offenders to state juvenile delinquency institutions (LEAA Indexed Legislative History, 1974). The removal of status offenders from the juvenile court became an important issue and is an interesting example of the community trying to cope with its ambivalence about whether delinquents should be treated as children or offenders.

The Removal of Status Offenders from Juvenile Court

Pressure to remove status offenders from juvenile court jurisdiction began to build even before the Supreme Court decisions that granted due process rights to juveniles. In 1961 the Second United Nations Congress on Prevention of Crime and Treatment of Offenders in London recommended that "the meaning of the term juvenile delinquency should be restricted as far as possible to violations of criminal law" (United Nations, 1961:61). In 1967, the President's Commission also recommended that "serious consideration should be given to complete elimination of the court's power over children for noncriminal conduct" (President's Commission, 1967:25). The National Task Force to Develop Standards and Goals for Juvenile Justice and Delinquency Prevention

took a similar position in 1977 (National Task Force, 1977:3), as did the framers
of the Juvenile Justice Standards developed by the Institute of Judicial Administration and the American Bar Association (Flicker, 1977:51).

Separation of status offenders from delinquents helped to ease the dilemma about whether delinquents were to be considered children or offenders, as the argument for separation had focused on the need to protect status offenders from the bad influences of delinquents and the stigma of court processing. However, by distinguishing delinquents as *offenders* who had committed an act which if committed by an adult would be a crime, and by separating them from noncriminal status offenders (or children in need of community protection), advocates of stricter handling of delinquents could tighten their control with less inhibition regarding their other status as children.

As Empey notes, somewhat ironically, the enthusiasm for keeping delinquents and status offenders separate is reminiscent of the enthusiasm exhibited by nineteenth century reformers when they sought to have children separated from the contaminating influence of adult offenders (Empey, 1980: 167). In the late 1960s, as many states revised their children's codes, status offenders who were separated from delinquents became known by a variety of euphemisms: In Colorado they were CHINS, or Children in Need of Supervision; in New York they were PINS, Persons in Need of Supervision; and in other states they were either JINS, Juveniles in Need of Supervision, or MINS, Minors in Need of Supervision.

After a flutter of legislative activity to separate these two types of offenders, some states moved to abolish status offenders altogether, motivated by the strong federal initiatives provided by the JJDP Act of 1974 as well as the continued concern about the stigma and coercive nature of any court appearance. There are good reasons to remove noncriminal offenders from the juvenile court, but the deletion of status offenders changes the character of the court and may substantially weaken attempts to consider the child status of delinquent.

It may also create a void in services for troubled children. There is some sentiment within juvenile courts (Polier, 1974:114) that status offenders often pose the most serious problems in the court. The juvenile court may not be the appropriate body to distribute child welfare services, but it has been associated with the "treatment" of problem youths for many years (Rothman, 1980:245; Ryerson, 1978:85; Schlossman, 1977:58), and it has tried to provide the concern and care of a good parent for the problem child. What agency, if any, will become responsible for this group of troubled and troubling children if the court divests itself of them?

Indeed, as status offenders are evicted from juvenile court, they seem to become invisible, and we must ask ourselves if their removal from the courts is a step forward in the protection of children or an abrogation of community responsibility for their welfare.

The Continuing Dilemmas

Throughout the history of juvenile justice in America, the courts have operated with ambiguous goals and an ambivalent citizenry. At its inception, the court negotiated a definition of its goals that included an emphasis on the juvenile's best interest, an emphasis on the youth's status as child rather than as offender, and an assumption that what was good for the child would be good for the community. Allen suggests (1964), that these goals and assumptions were probably never shared fully by the community. The disagreement among contemporary scholars about whether the early court reformers were attempting to control and exploit the children of the "dangerous" lower classes or were genuinely committed to helping them probably reflects the existence of *both* perspectives within the reform movement. This duality of purpose may have diluted the effectiveness of reformers and may be one reason why the court was never able to garner the necessary resources and support it needed for success. The difficulty in deciding whose "best interest" and whose understanding of "best interest" should prevail has plagued the court from its beginning.

In fact, the court's lack of clarity regarding procedures and goals, combined with a wide latitude of organizational and individual discretion, yielded an environment in which units in the court network were able to press their own goals rather than the court's. In attempting to make the juvenile offender's child status the overriding consideration, for example, the early court did not allow for a systematic discussion of the conflicts and responses engendered by the child's offender status. As a result, there was wide variation in decisions made within and between courts, and a growing concern about the juvenile court's ability to respond appropriately to either status.

The early belief that troubled and troublesome juveniles could be successfully handled in a system based on altruism and maximum discretion has failed to yield results generally believed to be satisfactory. In light of the conflicting ideologies about juvenile offenders and the ambiguous structure of the juvenile courts, this is not surprising. The early court did not provide a structure that admitted the existence of conflicting goals, even though they may have existed, so no systematic and realistic attempt was made to set priorities.

Without priorities and legal guidelines, it was difficult for the community to monitor the use of discretion.

The present emphasis on due process in juvenile court can be seen in part as a response to the continuing ambiguity about the role of the court. Due process, already well established in criminal courts, represents something of a consensus about how people accused of crime should be treated. As a kind of universally accepted standard, it protects the court from charges of arbitrariness as well as from charges of undue attention to the child status of an offender. As we have seen, the transition to due process in juvenile court has been an essential one, but it is not the end point in the struggle for meaningful justice for juveniles.

The hopes that due process would resolve important problems of the juvenile court have not been fulfilled. The legal procedures now common in juvenile courts have not guaranteed justice for children, just as they have failed to always assure justice for adults. As the juvenile court comes to resemble a mini-criminal court, some scholars are beginning to ask whether we need a specialized juvenile court at all (e.g., Feld, 1984).

The court's dream, representing such high goals and optimism about the ability of a society to care for its children, has become tarnished in part because there was never just one dream of justice for juveniles, but many dreams and many purveyors of dreams. This ideological mix influenced and continues to influence the context in which specific juvenile courts operate.

The remaining chapters in this book describe how individuals and agencies within one court attempted to negotiate the many dreams of juvenile justice and how they competed for the community's scarce resources. The purpose here is not to predict outcomes, but rather to draw attention to the complexity of a court's environment, and to describe how court participants may negotiate ideologies and resources in reaching decisions about the general nature of a court and the individual decisions it makes. Hopefully, as we come to better understand the court's history and ongoing dilemmas, we will be better able to chart a realistic course for its future.

3

A Court in Its Context

The Place: Suburban County

Suburban County, like many suburban communities in high growth areas in the United States, is undergoing major change, feeling the press of rapid population increase combined with an overloaded and decentralized system of service delivery (SYP, 1105). The county is long and thin, and its size and shape play an important role in its ability to deliver services and consolidate resources. It lies at the edge of a large metropolitan area and includes both high-growth communities with substantial populations and rural areas dominated by rolling expanses of prairie and dirt roads.

The population of Suburban County nearly doubled over the decade from 1970 to 1980, when it reached a high of almost 300,000. The overall population growth added roughly 16,500 children to the community (SYP, 1105). The county had no reserve of facilities to meet the needs of these children. An established neighborhood with fluctuations in population may have underutilized buildings and services in place that can be upgraded to accommodate a surge in population; a new area has none, and must build from the ground up.

For the most part, the population in the county is white and middle class—but demography in the eastern and western portions of the county differs. Many residents of the eastern portion of the county are classified as low-income or minority, whereas the western portion of the county includes some of the wealthiest communities in the state. Agency staff members who work in both areas talk of the "two different counties" they serve. Many find that programs successful in the west are inappropriate for clients in the east, and vice versa (SYP, 63).

Decentralization is a major characteristic of Suburban County. It has ten police departments (ranging in size from 17 to 125 persons), seven school districts, and nine municipalities that vary in size and have different histories and growth patterns. Each has its own ordinances that affect juveniles. Some have special juvenile units; others do not.

The county seat and most of the government and administrative offices are located in the western end of the county, where the population was concentrated during the early development of the county. The three-story 1907 brick building that houses juvenile court and other courtrooms looks like the stereotypic image of a small-town American courthouse. The wood paneled courtroom, has a distinctly modern look. Next to the courtroom are the judge's chambers, the clerk's office, and an open area with two adjoining smaller rooms for consultations. Youths and their families wait their turn on folding chairs in a hallway outside the courtroom.

The court operates roughly from 8:30 to 5:00 with an hour and a half for lunch. Mondays generally are reserved for trials, Tuesdays and Thursdays for a variety of non-trial proceedings in delinquency cases, and Wednesdays for dependency/neglect hearings. Fridays are set aside for more complicated delinquency cases.

The main offices for probation and diversion are next door to the court house, but like many of the government agencies in the county, they maintain branch offices in the eastern sector of the country as well. This can be an inconvenience to staff members who must shuttle back and forth across the county to attend meetings, and appear in court. Travel time often results in less time available for direct service for the children.

Travel is indeed a problem for everyone. Some court workers feel that decisions about services are based more on location than a child's needs. The relative placement of shelter and detention facilities, for example, may influence a police officer's decision about whether a child needs a secure facility. Other

factors being equal, the officer may decide in favor of a detention center if it   35
is close to the precinct and the juvenile court, rather than a shelter 25 miles
away on the far side of the county.

History: Suburban Court Over Twenty Years

The state in which Suburban County is located has been in the forefront of
juvenile justice reform since the beginning of the national juvenile court movement. Its revised juvenile code, to which Suburban Court's first long-term
juvenile judge made substantial contributions, was adopted in 1967 and anticipated the rights set forth in the *Gault* decision.

From County Court to District Court

In 1961, when juveniles were still handled by county courts, the Suburban
County judge handled 235 juvenile cases, while the county juvenile probation
officer handled cases of dependency/neglect, truants, and runaways in which
there was no legal action taken. Youths who required detention were either
transported to a nearby county or housed with the probation officer, who
took in 38 youths during the year (SYPN, 1A) in the spirit of the early juvenile
court's commitment to meeting the individual needs of children on a direct
and personal level. At that time, the county claimed to have the lowest juvenile
delinquency record in the state (SYPN, 1A).

In 1965, juvenile courts were moved from county jurisdiction to district
courts, which substantially upgraded them. The change increased the status
and pay of juvenile judges, facilitated appeals directly to the Supreme Court,
and concentrated services for juveniles in 22 judicial districts rather than in the
62 counties (Rubin, 1984). (Suburban County became part of a judicial district
that included three other counties, all primarily rural.) Until this change occurred, a single county judge heard juvenile cases only one day a week. Under
the new organization, four judges heard juvenile cases in rotation, but this
yielded inconsistent dispositions until ultimately the chief judge again consolidated all juvenile cases under one judge (SYP, 814). The man who became
the juvenile judge served for ten years, and left an indelible mark upon the
court. After he retired in 1975, the court went through a period of less consistent direction, with several judges rotating through the court until the appointment of the present judge in August 1977 (SYP, 711).

As the court grew, detention facilities also moved from local funding and control to consolidation within a state agency, changing considerably in size and scope. The county acquired its first juvenile detention facility in mid-1962, when it purchased a two-story frame house in the western sector of the county (SYPN, 1A). It provided an alternative to housing youths overnight with the probation officer or transporting them to a detention center in a neighboring county. Court employees pitched in to paint and prepare the building for its first occupants (SYP, 814). The center enabled the court to keep local youngsters close to their own homes and separate from the "tougher" adolescents in the detention facility in the nearby city.

Four years later the county remodeled another building to serve as its first "juvenile evaluation center" (later called the Youth Detention Center). In 1970, the funding of the detention center shifted from the county to the State Judicial Department. In 1973, it shifted again to the State Division of Youth Services, Department of Institutions (SYP, 814).

Probation Services

Funding for juvenile probation facilities also shifted from the county to the state. In 1970, the State's Judicial Department assumed responsibility for funding probation services, which in Suburban County included three probation officers and a chief probation officer (SYP, 1106). Within a year, the juvenile staff had increased to seven and a half workers, where it stabilized with little additional increase despite doubling of the county's population during the 1970s.

Originally, the probation department handled both adult and juvenile offenders, but in 1976, a separate juvenile division was created, headed by a juvenile probation supervisor who answered to the Chief Probation Officer.

Report on County Youth Services

In 1974 Suburban Court came under attack in a statewide Department of Institutions report on detention centers and shelter facilities. The report, prepared by a young lawyer for the state Department of Institutions, blasted the county's lack of detention services, as well as the attitudes of public officials, parents, citizens, and county commissioners (SYP, 1123).

Suburban County was one of the richest counties in the United States, she noted, but in "the most desperate need of reform of any of the counties

in the region" (SYP, 1126, 1131). She further claimed that frustration and   37
disgust about existing services and attitudes was more apparent among youth-
serving professionals in Suburban County than in any other county. One
worker she quoted described the county as "a sopping rich community which
doesn't give a damn about its children" (SYP, 1126). Another quoted county
commissioners as saying that, "the state will deal with the problems of our
children if we let things deteriorate enough" (SYP, 1131).

The report detailed problems with the existing detention center, including overcrowded, inadequate facilities; parental unwillingness to take kids
home from detention or to deal with their problems; and insufficient numbers
of nonsecure facilities. It also charged that the county detained a high percentage of status offenders, allowed 95 percent of detained youths to waive
detention hearings, and held youths for a longer average number of days (10)
than any place else in the state. The charges were essentially accurate, but
county officials felt their detention situation had been unfairly described. The
detention center, although technically for detention, had been used for several
years primarily as a place for status offenders to live while they waited for
placement. Staffed by houseparents rather than counselors, it was a "family
type of place" (SYP, 1049). It was a carry-over from the earlier philosophy
of juvenile justice that stressed treatment and removal of children from "un-
healthy" homes. By 1974, it was outdated by the more due process oriented
approach to juveniles and had become inadequate for the court's growing
population.

The report galvanized the county into action and temporarily focused a
great deal of attention on juvenile justice. It remained a sore point in the county
for years and was still referred to with some rancor in 1980–82. The county
commissioners responded by establishing a citizen's Commission on Youth
Services, funded with $1,000, to survey youths, parents, and agencies and
make recommendations to the budget committee and the county commissioners. It is unclear what long-term impact this action had, however. The
Commission recommended that a comprehensive plan for youth services be
developed in the county, but it was then dissolved.

In 1976, $92,460 was budgeted to establish a twenty-three member Youth
Services Council (YSC), which developed its own plan for youth services in
the county, published in October 1976. The plan recommended, among other
things, the relocation of the detention center by December 1977 (SYP, 1055).
Apparently, these recommendations were received with less than unanimous
enthusiasm, and soon afterward, the council acquired a wider scope of responsibilities and was renamed the Human Resources Council (HRC) (SYPN,
15). Youth advocates suggested that the county commissioners were unhappy

with the reports and plans of the Commission for Youth Services and the Youth Services Council and that they were responsible for the demise of both; in any event, neither the YSC nor the HRC played an effective role in the juvenile justice network.

The District Attorney responded to the 1974 report, by establishing a Justice Task Force in 1974 composed of representatives from police departments and agencies dealing with juveniles in the county (SYP, 42). The task force met once a month to evaluate the services available to juveniles and formulate ways to fill gaps when services were lacking or nonexistent. In 1980, it was discontinued due to lack of participation.

The district attorney also initiated a Juvenile Diversion Program, which got underway in 1975 and was funded initially with federal Juvenile Justice Delinquency Prevention funds. The program provided supervision and counseling for first-time or nonviolent offenders as an alternative to having their cases filed in court. After federal funding ended, the program continued using state and local monies (SYP, 42). In March, 1979, it opened a second office in the east side of the county and both were still in operation in 1982.

The report precipitated a variety of other programs as well. A shelter care home was established to provide a nonsecure alternative to the detention center, an interagency crisis intervention team was created to work with status offenders, and a group home for status offenders was opened.

Some trends are worth noting in the history of Suburban Court: First is the general movement from local to state control as the court was reclassified from a county to a district court, and probation and detention facilities moved from county to state funding and responsibility. These changes provided more resources for the court, but also reduced autonomy and local control. A second trend concerns the ever-spiraling population growth and a lack of clear direction for handling it. The growing population continually increased pressure on a court system that received only sporadic infusions of new resources.

The Legal System

Suburban Court operates within the state Juvenile Code, a progressive and comprehensive document that represents several years of revising and codifying. All rights extended to juveniles in recent major Supreme Court decisions are embodied in it, and it undergoes continual modification to keep pace with changes in juvenile justice on the national as well as the local scene.

Two major changes occurred in mid-1979. The first removed most status offenders from the court's delinquency jurisdiction, in compliance with 1974

federal legislation mentioned in Chapter 2. Children previously handled under
the old status offender designation came to be dealt with as dependency and
neglect cases, and essentially vanished from the court.

The second bill mandated alternatives to out-of-home placement and
aroused considerable controversy, confusion, and discussion at all levels of the
juvenile justice system. It emphasized the reduction of out-of-home placement
of children by granting greater control and flexibility to local communities in
regard to children's services, and required court review of all out-of-home
placements (SYP, 1144). Chapter 5 deals with this legislation in detail and
much of the rest of this book is about the changes created by the legislation,
in particular the changes its implementation created in Suburban Court's external and internal environment.

The Court Population

During the year of our study, the prosecutor received 1,586 requests to file
petitions in juvenile court, and actually filed 906 petitions, or 57 percent. The
rest he refused, took no action on, or diverted.[1] Our two study populations
included 710 youths who had one or more petitions filed in court and 452
youths who were initially referred to the District Attorney's Diversion Program.[2] Of the 452 diversion referrals, 130 were returned to the prosecutor for
further action by him, presumably the filing of a petition. The 710 youths
upon whom petitions were filed plus the 322 who remained in diversion make
up a total study population of approximately 1,032 youths.[3] Of these 1,032
youths, 44 percent were initially diverted by the prosecutor and 31 percent
actually remained in diversion.

The general affluence and homogeneity of the county suggest that the
court's population should have been predominately Anglo; in large part it was.
But the county also contained pockets of poverty and its boundaries were
adjacent to heavily populated areas of other counties with larger minority
populations. Court records showed a high proportion of youths who were
not residents of Suburban County. Although the records did not include information on race or socioeconomic status, court observation suggested that
there was a higher percentage of minority and lower income youths than one
would have expected from the overall demographics of Suburban County.
More detailed exploration of these two population characteristics raised some
interesting issues concerning the court's handling of nonresidents and its con-
centration of youths from lower income areas.

The court records showed that almost a third of the youths who entered the court network lived outside Suburban County. Residents and nonresidents were similar in many ways; they had similar charges, prior records, and background characteristics (Mahoney, A., 1987). Nonresident offenders were less likely to get dispositions that would utilize local resources. They were not as likely as residents for example, to be referred to the diversion program, and when they were, they averaged fewer meetings with their counselors (Mahoney, A., 1987). Often, after adjudication, nonresidents were granted a change of venue and sent back to their home court for disposition, a common practice throughout the state. But nonresidents whose cases stayed in court were more likely to be dismissed or to get a disposition that carried a lower cost to the local community, like a fine or commitment to the state Department of Institutions.

It was not possible to compare the court outcomes for residents and nonresidents because we were not able to follow up on the dispositions of nonresidents with change of venue. We suspect, however, that many nonresident youths fall through the cracks between court systems and do not receive the sanctions or treatments that their behavior may warrant.

Lower-Income Youth

Clients of urban courts are often from lower-income backgrounds (Spergel, 1976:63; Hasenfeld and Cheung, 1985:808), usually because American cities include substantial lower-income populations.

We assumed, given Suburban County's population, that its clients would be predominately white and middle class, and yet a disproportionate percentage were not. In order to see if proportionately more of the court's clients came from the lower-income pockets of the county, we plotted the addresses of all youths who had been through the court or diversion program on a map of the 63 census tracts in the county. For each tract, we calculated the percentage of youths who entered the court by comparing the number of youths aged 10 to 17 who lived in the tract with the number of youths it sent to court in 1980. From census records we obtained current housing values for tracts and categorized each one as having low, medium, or high housing values. The percentage of youths going to court per tract ranged from a low of below 1 percent to a high of 6 percent, with most tracts sending between 1 and 3 percent of their youths to court in 1980. Twelve tracts stood out as having either especially high or especially low percentages of adolescents entering the court system. Eight tracts had percentages higher than 3 percent, and four had percentages below 1 percent.

Table
3.1

Census tracts with either a high or low percentage of youths aged 10 to 17 entering   41
Suburban County's Juvenile Justice System and housing values of the tracts

Tract classification on housing value	% Youths enter system	% Residences valued over $100,000	% Residences valued under $50,000
L	6%	<1%	60%
L	6%	1%	52%
LM	5%	<1%	34%
LM	5%	1%	40%
LM	5%	<1%	31%
M	4%	3%	22%
HM	4%	47%	4%
M	4%	1%	2%
HM	<1%	47%	4%
H	<1%	98%	<1%
H	<1%	88%	<1%
M	<1%	3%	<1%

Based on 1980 census information.
L = modal category of housing valued under $50,000;
M = modal category of housing valued at $50,000 to $99,999;
H = modal category of housing valued at $100,000 or over;
LM = in M category, over 30% of houses were in low category;
HM = in M category, over 30% of houses were in high category.

Table 3.1 shows that the two tracts with the highest percentage of youths entering Suburban Court have low housing valuations (i.e., modal valuation under $50,000) and the tracts with the lowest percentage of youths have high or medium housing valuations (i.e., modal valuations over $100,000 or from $50,000 to $99,000). This is admittedly a crude measure of economic status, but if we assume that low housing valuations are indicative of lower-income areas and high valuations are indicative of high-income areas, we can speculate that Suburban Court youths are coming disproportionately from the county's low-income districts.

How does this unequal distribution occur? Is it that higher-status residents are less likely to get in trouble, or that the system is more likely to pull lower-status residents into the system? Research by Bozinovski and Fenster (1983) suggests the latter. According to their study, police officers in more affluent communities were more likely than officers in lower-income areas to try to negotiate a resolution of the problem between juveniles, parents, and victims. It appears that youths in Suburban County, as in other communities, are differentially at risk for court involvement depending on their socioeconomic level (Carter and Lohman 1968:20; Cicourel 1968:331; Thornberry 1973:97).

Characteristics of Youths in Suburban Court

Youths in Suburban Court, as in other jurisdictions, were more likely to be male than female, and averaged slightly over 15 years old. Less than half lived with both parents.[4] Most had only one petition against them and had been arrested for property crimes, most commonly theft (35 percent) or burglary (22 percent). Their victims were usually businesses, residences, or schools. Only 14 percent of the youths were charged with personal offenses.[5] Although over half the youths initially had felony charges, this was more a function of local practice than a measure of the seriousness of the behavior. Burglaries were always first charged as felonies in this court, as were more than three-quarters of the vandalism acts and forgeries.

It was difficult to get information about previous records. During 1980, Suburban Court began to utilize the Prosecutors' Management Information System (PROMIS), a computer system for keeping and checking arrest records across jurisdictions. It did not include records from one large bordering jurisdiction (SYPN, 67A), however. Given the mobility of local youths, this sharply limited its usefulness. Information about previous offenses was available for only 25 percent of the 710 youths in the study, and half of these indicated that the offender had no records. Most of the 92 youths who had previous records had been charged with property offenses and had more than two recorded offenses (68 percent). Twelve percent had eight or more.

The Network: Other County Institutions

Suburban County schools, social services, and courts share many of the same clients. Shifts in funding priorities brought a restructuring of their relationships in regard to juveniles.

Schools

Interactions between Suburban Court and the community's seven school systems had been tense for years. The schools were feeling the impact of a rapidly expanding population and of decentralization, and student enrollments were

uneven, growing rapidly in the newer housing developments on the east side   43
of the county and declining in some of the long-established western neigh-
borhoods. Older residents in the west, with fewer children, were less likely
to approve bond issues and tax increases to expand facilities in the new areas
(SYPN, 223). As a result, some districts found it increasingly difficult to
provide adequate school facilities. (This will be discussed more fully in
Chapter 7.)

   A recent federal law (Public Law 94–142) put acute pressure on schools
to develop special education programs. Under this statute, schools were required to conduct "child find" activities, that is, to locate and serve children
in need of services. But schools feared the potential drain on resources that a
large pool of children with special needs might create (Jacobs, 1985:3) and
were wary of any cooperative arrangements that might further expand the
population of handicapped learners for which they might be financially responsible. The juvenile court posed a particular threat, since youths who found
their way into court often had done badly in school and many were believed
by court workers to have learning disabilities (Magnetti, 1982). Schools already
under financial stress were not eager to take on the additional cost of educating
juvenile delinquents, under the new federal mandate.

   The Board of Cooperative Education Services (BOCES), representing
five of the school districts in Suburban County, had planning and services
arrangements with Suburban Court. Representatives from BOCES sat on the
county's interagency Placement Alternatives Commission (PAC) for juvenile
offenders, and in these and other meetings there were strong disagreements
over who should decide if a child needed "special education" and who should
assume the cost. This tension was an important dimension of Suburban Court's
context with implications for policy, resources, and decisions regarding delinquents; it is discussed at length in later chapters.

Social Services

The court, although ostensibly autonomous, was highly dependent on Social
Services because the latter's foster care budget paid for all residential programs
used by the court except commitments to the state Department of Institutions
and mental health placements. As resources for placement declined, competition between the court and social services for control of placement decisions
increased. This competition was played out in several arenas—was a focal
point of interaction in the court network over the year. It will be discussed in
detail in Chapters 6 and 7.

   The social services department was under organizational stress on several fronts. It was attempting to cope with the financial impact of new legislation to limit out-of-home placement which restructured its financial arrangements with the state. It faced new licensing requirements for residential child care facilities that threatened to close several existing facilities and further limit the range of placement choice for children (SYP, 163). Its rapidly expanding welfare and foster care budgets were running into strong opposition from local county commissioners. Finally, its staff suffered such rapid turnover that a caseworker rarely handled a given court case from beginning to end.

Municipal Court

Into the already complex set of interorganizational networks that included schools, social services, mental health services, police departments and the juvenile court, came the Suburban County municipal courts. In Suburban County and throughout the state prior to 1979, they had been prohibited from having any involvement with juveniles. In 1980, however, this changed, but not without months of organizational and legal machinations. In 1979, a new ruling by the State Court of Appeals held that the juvenile court did not have exclusive jurisdiction over children aged 10 to 18 unless the child had violated a state law or municipal ordinance that carried a jail sentence (SYP, 1154). The new ruling opened jurisdiction over juveniles to courts other than the juvenile court as long as no jail sentence was imposed. As a result, towns and cities in Suburban County moved quickly to extend their control over teenagers by eliminating jail sentences for a variety of offenses despite the objection of children's rights advocates, who argued that case processing would be too fast and that special needs would not be identified and children's rights not protected.

One city in a high-population area of the county was particularly eager for this kind of municipal court control. In 1979, almost 50 percent of its arrests involved juvenile offenders, but as long as exclusive jurisdiction for juveniles was vested in the Juvenile Court, it had little control over the speed or severity of their disposition (SYPN, 98). Officers complained that the juvenile court process took too long and that they could do nothing but lecture and release youths for minor offenses (SYPN, 98).

On the other hand, the municipal courts' control over juvenile offenders had some serious problems connected with it, which worried court officials and child advocates. Because it could get its new authority only by giving up jail sentences, the court was left without any way to enforce penalties: If a youth refused to pay a fine, for example, the municipal court judge could do nothing but levy another one. One city council suggested an ordinance that

permitted a maximum 90 day jail sentence for contempt of court for juveniles   45
between 10 and 18 who failed to appear in court, did not pay a fine, or otherwise
flaunted the court's authority. The proposal brought a storm of protest.

Finally, after many proposals and counter proposals, the council unanimously agreed on an ordinance that allowed the jailing of youths over 16 for
contempt for a maximum of five days (SYPN, 124). The ordinance was ar-
guably in violation of the state children's code, and courts were not quick to
test its legality. Three months after the ordinance went into effect, a local
newspaper reported that no jail sentence had yet been imposed on a juvenile
by a municipal judge (SYPN, 163).

After much lobbying and discussion, the state Children's Code was modified by the state legislature in 1981 to allow a municipal court judge to impose
a 48-hour jail sentence on a juvenile for any kind of contempt of court. The
jail sentence had to be served in a detention facility operated by or contracted
with the Youth Services Division of the state Department of Institutions, if
one was available within 40 miles of the court (SYP, 937, 1148). Although
child advocates continued to disapprove of the use of jail sentences by municipal
courts, they came to view them as almost inevitable in the growing conservative climate and hailed the final provisions for short and carefully restricted
sentences as almost a victory.

It was hard to know what short-range impact the new municipal ordinances had on the juvenile court. Workers from the Juvenile Diversion Program worried that municipal court would drain clients from its already underutilized programs (SYP, 568). Other court officials worried that the municipal
probation program in one city would expand court interference into children's
lives. Critics questioned whether municipal courts could continue to process
cases rapidly and offer meaningful probation if they were forced to contend
with the large numbers of juveniles who had been previously lectured and
released or sent to juvenile court (SYP, 586).

The short-term effects of the municipal court's movement into juvenile
justice proved to be less noticeable than had been expected. Supervisors in the
Juvenile Diversion Program said they felt an initial decrease in cases during
the summer, after the ordinances had been passed, but our analysis of the
referrals to the diversion program did not show a clear downward trend. There
was a slight downward dip in summer and early fall, but then referrals showed
an upward swing again at the end of the year (SYP, 1155).

Long-term effects of the change may ultimately show more juveniles
sanctioned for their behavior—which may be good if it gives them a stronger
sense of not being able to get away with petty offenses. Municipal court
jurisdiction may be bad, however, if it pulls more juveniles into the court

unnecessarily, labels them inappropriately, or trivializes the court process through hearings that are too quick and peremptory.

Over time, municipal handling of juveniles may change the population of Suburban Court as minor offenses are screened from it and it is left with mostly serious or repeat offenders. This change will undoubtedly require re-thinking of the court's role, procedures, and dispositional alternatives.

Municipal court handling of juveniles is a victory of local autonomy over state control. It returns the handling of minor juvenile offenders to the community, a control largely lost when juveniles were put in the centralized state operated District Courts. State legislation specifying the conditions under which juveniles can be jailed, however, provides state limitations on local power. This mix of state and local responsibility illustrates the ways in which levels of government can work together to handle problems and populations shared by both. It opens possibilities for both increased tension and increased co-operation.

A Changing Framework

During the year we observed, not only were there environmental changes involving new legislation, funding shifts, and organizational constellations within the county, but also a variety of changes at the individual level. Personnel changes in the offices of the public defender and prosecutor kept daily operations in the courtroom in almost constant flux. Several public defenders made numerous demands not made by previous public attorneys. Several new prosecutors passed through the court as well, also with attendant disruptions. Probation officers generally found new prosecutors difficult, regardless of their style, because they always wanted more information on juveniles than more experienced prosecutors and required more formal written reports, thus substantially increasing probation's work load.

Although the probation staff had been more stable than the other agencies, it too underwent several personnel changes during the year, as well as a major reorganization the following year when the separate boundaries between the juvenile and adult divisions were wiped out. Before the reorganization, probation officers worked with either juvenile or adult case loads and handled both predisposition investigation and supervision so they could stay with the same client throughout the process. After the reorganization, all probation officers handled both adults and juveniles and specialized in either predisposition investigation or supervision. The special character and rapport of the juvenile probation unit fell away. The juvenile supervisor, who had been very involved and influential in all aspects of the juvenile justice network over many 47 years, turned his attention elsewhere as he took over supervision of predisposition reports for both adults and juveniles.

The biggest change in Suburban Court, and one widely welcomed in spite of the logistical problems it caused, was the addition of a new juvenile court judge at the beginning of 1981. The new judge took over all cases with east side addresses (about a third of the docket) and began hearing cases in her east side courtroom. Suddenly the court had two courtrooms, widely separated, with no new staff. Agencies found themselves even more thinly spread than before. The two district attorneys traveled several times a week to the east side court and the one juvenile public defender balanced the two courtrooms as best she could. Probation abandoned the practice of keeping an officer in court to provide information on cases and meet with newly referred juveniles.

After six months, just as things were settling into a routine, the two judges swapped courtrooms, taking their court staff with them. Long-term work relationships were disrupted as clerical staffs in the west side court tried to adjust to a new juvenile clerk who, in turn, tried to cope with a new clerical staff. This was one more example of the constant change going on in the court and its related agencies.

Suburban Court is an intricate network tied into a complex environment staffed with mobile individuals. Its character is shaped by its location and by its population. The court network cooperated and competed with other agencies in the community as it tried to cope with new legislation and funding priorities as well as daily disruptions created by high personnel turnover. Writing a book about Suburban Court and its context is like trying to take a snapshot of a rapidly growing and highly active child who never holds still.

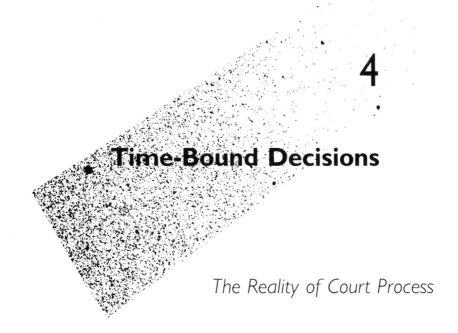

4

Time-Bound Decisions

The Reality of Court Process

The Importance of Time in Juvenile Court

Time is an important resource for any court. If a court cannot dispose of cases at a reasonable rate, a backlog arises, and unless something is done to reduce the imbalance, the backlog continues to grow and individual cases take longer and longer to move from arrest to final disposition. Courts cope with this problem by increasing personnel or by using more efficiently the time and resources already available. (A court can also temporarily increase resources in order to reduce a backlog and then drop back to the previous resource level, which may be adequate once the backlog has been cleared away.)

Time has a special meaning in juvenile court. The court's three primary objectives—rehabilitation in the best interests of the child, protection of the community, and fairness of process—must be carried out within a limited time frame. The more days the court spends in processing a youth's case, the fewer it has left for treatment. It is also important because youths are generally less able than adults to anticipate the future and cope with delays. Their perspectives on offenses and treatment may change over months or even weeks (Goldstein, Freud, and Solnit, 1973:40). Also because adolescents are in the midst of rapid developmental changes, any substantial delay during a critical stage of their learning process can have important consequences for their continued maturation (Kohlberg and Kramer, 1969).

Four Kinds of Time

In order to understand some of the issues regarding time in Suburban Court, it is useful to think about several different elements of time within the court system. Most of the literature on time in courts focuses on case processing time, but there are other ways of thinking about time as a resource. The four perspectives on time—court time, case time, defendant time, and intervention time—focus attention on different aspects of the court's role (Mahoney, A., 1985a).

Court Time

Court time is the time available to the court each day to deal with the cases on that session's calendar. The more cases there are in a court, the more cases there are to compete for available staff time. Caseloads in juvenile courts may be influenced by a variety of factors, including new community facilities and demographics. For example, the opening in a jurisdiction of a new shopping mall that attracts teenagers may drive up caseloads. Rapid population growth in an area also can bring an increasing number of adolescents into a jurisdiction.

The use of court time may be even more problematic in juvenile court than it is in adult court because the necessary cast of participants for a hearing, in addition to the accused child, may include parents, social service workers, probation officers, guardians ad litem, representatives of previous or current placement agencies, and school officials. Assembling the necessary people and the relevant files can prove logistically difficult, and often requires frequent adjournments or waiting periods at the court.

Structural arrangements, including such due process requirements as advisement of rights and other rituals of the adversary process, took a lot of Suburban Court's time. Because juveniles are minors and believed to be under the protection of the court in a way that adults are not, there is particular

concern about whether they understand procedures and are competent to waive   51
rights and make decisions.

Case Time

Case time reflects the court's role in administering timely justice. The court is
responsible to the community for bringing children to a public accounting for
their behavior within a reasonable period of time.

Recent summaries of research on court processing times and on implementation of delay reduction programs (Church, et al., 1978a; Levin, 1975;
B. Mahoney, Sipes, and Ito, 1985; Mahoney, Winberry, Church, 1981; Neubauer, et al., 1980) show that for adult courts, case processing time is influenced
by such contextual or system factors as general court culture, community
environment, case volume, procedural requirements, resource constraints, adjournment practices, the effectiveness of a court's scheduling and listing procedures, and utilization of available court time. Both speed and backlog are
determined in significant measure by established expectations, practices, and
informal rules of behavior of judges and attorneys as court systems adapt to
a given pace of litigation.

Standards for juvenile case processing time have recently been adopted
by several national groups, including the American Bar Association (1984) and
the Conference of State Court Administrators (1983), and all are comparable
in their recommendations for juvenile courts. For example, all of the standards
provide that a detained youth should have a detention hearing within 24 hours
of admission and an adjudicatory or transfer hearing within 15 days of admission. In addition, they stipulate that an undetained juvenile should have
an adjudicatory or transfer hearing within 30 days of the filing of the petition
and a dispositional hearing within 15 days of the adjudicatory hearing, unless
the court grants additional time in exceptional cases (ABA, 1984; Melcher,
1984:49; Moran, 1984). The Institute of Judicial Administration and American
Bar Association (IJA-ABA) Standards also set limits for pretrial proceedings.
Section 2.2 in the volume on Pretrial Court proceedings notes that the initial
appearance of a delinquency respondent before a judge of the juvenile court
should not be later than five days after the petition has been filed (IJA-ABA,
1980c).

Accompanying the emphasis on time standards is a growing awareness
of the importance of management information, e.g. information on the age
and status of pending cases. Without such information it is difficult to know
how serious the time problem is, what the key issues are, and whether efforts

to reduce delay are working (Mahoney, B., and Sipes, 1985:9). It was only in 1986, however, that these problems began to be addressed systematically in juvenile courts. The Institute for Court Management, in its June 1986 workshop on Managing Cases in Juvenile Courts, noted, "The Institute has conducted many workshops on caseflow management and delay reduction. This is the first to focus exclusively on improving case management in juvenile and family courts." (Institute for Court Management, 1986)

Child Time

Child time focuses on the child's perspective on the court's use of time, and draws our attention to the *quality* of time that is given to court appearances. Since court appearance is the only contact most arrested youths have with the court, their impression of the fairness of their treatment and the effectiveness of any sanctions imposed on them may rest on their perception of those few moments before the judge (Baum and Wheeler, 1968; Studt, 1961).

In attempting to get a sense of child time, we must try to understand how the court hearing appears from the child's perspective. How are the objectives of the court made clear to the youthful offender? As procedures become increasingly routine, it is also important to consider how much substance there is in a court appearance. What is the ratio of ritual (such as recitation of legal rights) to substance, and is the ritual as important to the youth as it is to members of the bar?

The atmosphere of the hearing has been a source of much controversy in the juvenile court since *Gault*. Many judges still maintain that an atmosphere of informality and parental concern is therapeutically valuable, but this kind of environment becomes more difficult to maintain as hearings move through a formal and prescribed pattern of legal steps.

Intervention Time

Intervention time concerns the point at which an individual who has gotten in trouble may be particularly amenable to change or treatment, and is especially relevant to juveniles given the premise of the "best interest of the child." Most theories of punishment emphasize the importance of prompt sanctions for undesirable behavior in order to maximize the sanction's impact in changing behavior (Walters, Park, and Cane, 1965). Despite the good intentions of judges and attorneys, however, intervention time is usually not a high priority in determining the speed of juvenile court proceedings.

The juvenile supervising probation officer in Suburban Court noted that probation officers generally found that the longer it took a child to go through the court, the more difficult it was to work with the child. He argued that anything beyond three months from offense to disposition was too long. The juvenile prosecutor also complained that delay complicated treatment and enabled adolescents to continue offending while their cases worked their way through court (SYP, 434,440). This view is reflected in time standards that are shorter for juveniles than for adults, for example, 30 days from the filing of a petition to adjudication for juveniles compared to 90 days from arrest to trial for adults accused of misdemeanors (Conference of State Court Administrators 1983; Stull, 1982).

Some defense attorneys argue, on the other hand, that delay in resolving a case can be good for some youths, who might use the time to show job or school accomplishments that reflect an ability to stay out of trouble. (The youth who can do this may be able to avoid a negative sanction beyond arrest and court appearance.) But although case delay may enable some youths to prove that they do not need intervention, the court and attorneys have difficulty justifying long case processing times for large numbers of youths on that basis. Rather than proving their reliability, many youths continue to get into trouble while their cases are pending, and as they build a record of offenses, they may find themselves eligible for out-of-home placement under the mandatory sentence statute for repeat offenders.

The Priority of Kinds of Time

Establishing priorities with respect to these four kinds of time is difficult. Efficiently processed cases usually result in a time-effective court; however, a court's push for efficiency can threaten to move cases to completion in a time *shorter* than our ideals of justice deem proper. For instance, emphasis on court time and case time may not be compatible with effective child time if a child needs personal attention, time-consuming explanations, or adjournments. And intervention time moves at its own highly individualized rate and may not be in harmony with anything that goes on in the legal system.

The tension resulting from trying to juggle these different kinds of time was obvious in Suburban Court. Analysis of case records shows that long case processing times were a problem for many Suburban Court youths. Yet observations and interviews suggest that there was no clear agreement about the best way to deal with delay, in part because of differing valuations of the different kinds of time. A description of the process of Suburban Court gives some sense of the experience of youths who go through the court and also shows how the court's finite resource, time, is gained and lost through its process.

Case Processing Time in Suburban Court

Table 4.1 shows the times in Suburban Court during 1980 for each phase of court processing.[1] Mean and median times are given, as well as the 75th percentile case and the range of time it took cases to move through six stages of processing: offense to apprehension, apprehension to filing, filing to advisement, advisement to adjudication, filing to adjudication,[2] and adjudication to disposition. It also shows how long it took cases to move all the way from filing to disposition and from apprehension to disposition.

Apprehension and Arrest

Most youths enter the juvenile court through police contact. A few, mostly residents who commit offenses in other jurisdictions, are sent to Suburban Court from other courts for sentencing. Our study picked up only youths who were referred to the prosecutor, so no information is available about the number or type of contacts the different police departments have with youths or the different ways they may use time. The larger departments have juvenile units and their own diversion programs. The smaller departments rely more heavily on informal conferences with parents and children.

The main options available to police officers include lecture and release (avoiding formal contact with any court), a summons to appear in municipal court (moving the child toward a lower level local court and away from the more centralized juvenile court), and taking a youth to the police station. At the station house, some youths are lectured, released, and sent home with their parents and/or referred to a diversion program or other community agency. More serious or repetitive offenders are officially booked. Because the prosecutor handles all court intake in Suburban Court, the police officer sends his report directly to the district attorney in charge of juvenile cases.

A study of all police reports that resulted either in a referral to the District Attorney's Diversion Program or a petition in court shows that the mean number of days from offense to apprehension is 12. In this instance the mean is increased by the long time periods for the 10 percent of youths who were at large for 30 days or longer.

Table 4.1   Case processing time by stage

Stage of process	Number of cases*	Range of days	Mean days	Median days	75th percentile case†
Offense to apprehension	683	0–350	12	0	5
Apprehension to filing	682	0–346	75	56	99
Filing to advisement	664	0–267	73	77	99
Advisement to adjudication	665	0–617	76	49	112
Filing to adjudication	699	0–784	158	119	205
Adjudication to disposition	400	0–314	32	0	56
Filing to disposition	397	0–488	155	135	209
Apprehension to disposition	391	0–756	218	197	284

*Total number = 710
†Number of days it takes the 75th percentile case to complete the stage

Apprehension to Filing

The district attorney reviews each police report, runs a record check on the youth, and decides whether to drop the case, refer it to the diversion program, or file a petition in court. Probation officers usually are not involved in cases until after they are adjudicated; the district attorney can request input from them, but rarely does unless a child is currently on probation.

In this phase of the process, time is split between the police and the prosecutor, and in our study there was no way to separate the police and prosecutor responsibility for moving cases. A prosecutor we talked with at the start of our research estimated that it took two months for a case to get to him after an offense was committed because of the time it took for police investigations and preparation of reports. After he received the case, moreover, it would often sit on his desk for days before he could look at it because he was the only juvenile prosecutor and spent most of his day in the courtroom (SYP, 1981:70).

After the prosecutor makes a decision about whether to file a case in juvenile court, it goes to a secretary in the prosecutor's office to be typed. From there the case goes to the court, where the court clerk's office must file the petition. This date then becomes the official date of filing.

The mean number of days between apprehension and filing of a case in Suburban Court was 75. Just over half of the cases (54%) were filed within 60 days, and over a quarter (29%) took from three months to nearly a year to be filed. It is important to realize that the filing of a case does not constitute a court appearance, but is simply the point at which the case officially enters the court system and is given a number.

Detention

In 1980, Suburban Court detained 17 percent of juveniles upon whom petitions were filed. Youths were held because they were believed to be a danger to themselves or others, because they had warrants against them, or because their parents could not be located or were unable or unwilling to take them home. Detained youths were required to have detention hearings within 48 hours of being taken into custody. After this hearing, just under half of the youths were released. A third of the remaining youths were released within two days and another third were out within one week. Eighteen percent of the detained youths stayed 50 days or longer.

Filing to Adjudication

The various time standards set for juveniles generally recommend a maximum of 30 days between filing of a petition and the adjudicatory hearing. Information on case processing times in twelve juvenile courts utilized in an Institute for Court Management Workshop in 1986 showed that many of the courts exceeded that. The median number of days for undetained youths to go from petition to arraignment ranged from 0 to 96.5 over the twelve courts. The median from arraignment to adjudication was 0 to 111.5 (Institute for Court Management, 1986). In Suburban Court, the median was 77 days for cases to move from filing the petition to advisement (arraignment) and 49 days from advisement to adjudication. These times put the court toward the extreme high end of the spectrum, even when we take into consideration that our method of calculation was based on individuals rather than cases and thus may show longer times.[3]

In part, the long wait between filing and advisement was created by a backlog that overloaded dockets so that new cases were scheduled weeks after 57 they were filed. Thus delay compounded delay; only 20 percent of the youths had their advisement hearing within 30 days of filing, and only an additional 16 percent had it within 60 days. This period between the filing of a petition and advisement is important, since key psychological and legal aspects of an offense cannot be fully addressed by a youth, his family, or his counselors until the youth has been officially notified of the charges against him.

Some youths in Suburban Court, especially first-time or minor offenders, moved their cases to a speedy end once they got to the advisement hearing. In general, they either appeared with counsel, or waived their right to counsel, and pleaded guilty. Some were given a reserved adjudication on the spot—a six-month informal probation which, if successfully completed, leads to case dismissal. Over half the youths in Suburban Court entered a plea at this first hearing and 16 percent were adjudicated at the same time. Youths who did not plead guilty at the first appearance stayed in the court much longer. The median number of days from advisement to adjudication was 49.

Some youths who pleaded guilty in the first hearing were nonresidents who were transferred to their home courts for sentencing. Others were referred to the probation department for a presentence evaluation and recommendation of appropriate sanctions.

The judge in Suburban Court strongly encouraged youths to get attorneys. Youths who appeared for advisement without attorneys yet wanted the opportunity to seek legal counsel were given a date for a later hearing called Appearance of Counsel (AOC). Over half, (55 percent) of the 664 Suburban Court youths upon whom information was available, did obtain legal counsel. Of these, most (69 percent) had private attorneys. (Many families in the community earned too much money to qualify for public defenders.)

Employees of the court insisted that youths who were represented by attorneys took longer to go through court than those who were not, and a comparison of the processing times of the two groups supports these observations. Among youths with one petition, and an accusation of burglary or theft for example, those with attorneys took, on the average, three times as long to move from filing to adjudication as youths without attorneys (74 mean days compared to 24 mean days). Among youths with two or more petitions, those with attorneys took 82 days to reach adjudication compared to 23 days for those without attorneys (Mahoney and Fenster, 1987). These differences remained even when the potential influence of other factors, such as the complexity of the case, were taken into consideration. The long processing times were not compensated for, as some authors (e.g., Lemert, 1970) suggest, by more positive case outcomes for youths represented by attorneys.

If initial efforts to plea-bargain are unsuccessful, the case is set for trial either before a judge or a jury of six, depending on the youth's preference. Of the 650 youths upon whom information is available, 14 percent (94) had their cases set for trial and 7 youths actually went to trial. Of these, four were found guilty and three were acquitted. Cases set for trial took considerably longer to move through the court than cases not set for trial, even when other factors were taken into consideration (an average of 233 days compared to 118 days). Over 70 percent of the cases set for trial were not resolved until on or after the date set for trial (Mahoney A., 1985b; 563).

Ultimately most youths who appeared in court pleaded guilty, but some went through several more hearings before doing so. If a case was not resolved within the first 30 to 40 days, it was likely to stay in the system a long time. The third quartile case was 112 days and 10 percent of the youths waited over 195 days to move from advisement to adjudication. Some cases were adjourned many times, and crowded dockets resulted in appearances being separated by weeks and months.

If a youth denied the allegations at the advisement hearing, the case was sent to a pre-trial conference in order to give the youth (and the defense counsel, if any) an opportunity to learn what evidence the prosecutor had against him or to negotiate or plea-bargain with the prosecutor to reach a mutually agreeable disposition. The type of plea-bargaining usually seen in Suburban Court entailed the dismissal of one or more counts in the petition in exchange for admissions to the remaining counts, or the dismissal of an entire petition in exchange for an admission to all or part of another petition. The dismissal of an entire petition was viewed as a useful concession since each adjudicated petition counts toward the three adjudications necessary for mandatory out-of-home placement.

Court Time vs. Child Time

Court time and child time are closely tied issues, and both influence case processing time from advisement to adjudication. The due process orientation of the court requires it to devote considerable effort to routine advisements and procedures, and these provide the court with a dilemma: Although advisements are a routine court procedure, they can be highly important to a youth, since youths who do not understand their rights cannot exercise them. Judges are charged with making these rights explicit, yet in doing so, they may find themselves repeating a set phrase dozens of times each day.

In Suburban Court, the judge believed that each youth should have his
or her moment in court, and, accordingly, he went through the advisement
of rights slowly and carefully with each child, pausing often to ask the child
if he or she understood. This kind of care in regard to the reading of rights,
and the daily effort to make it sound fresh and important for each child, was
impressive. But individual advisement of rights became a tedious and time-
consuming exercise given the ever-increasing number of cases on the docket
(SYP, 584). Consequently, there was disagreement throughout the course of
our study over how to reconcile the importance of careful description of rights
with the importance of expeditious movement of cases through the court.

Disposition

Once a youth's guilt was established, the court moved fairly quickly to sentencing and final resolution, although the mean number of days between
adjudication and disposition (32) was still higher than the 15 days recommended
by the standards and higher than that of most of the 12 courts in the Institute
for Court Management Workshop. Cases in Suburban Court took an average
of 135 days to move from filing to disposition. This was considerably higher
than the average of 49.3 reported for juvenile cases in 27 state and local jurisdictions in a study by the National Center for Juvenile Justice (National Center
for State Courts, 1985).

More than half (56%) of the 400 youths who received dispositions were
sentenced at the same time they were adjudicated.[4] Over a quarter of all youths
(28 percent) pleaded guilty and were given reserved adjudication, usually considered the most lenient disposition because it includes dismissal of the case if
the six-month probationary period is successfully completed. Youths who
violated the terms of their reserved adjudication were adjudicated as delinquents and became subject to the full range of dispositional alternatives.

The variety of dispositions for adjudicated delinquents was not great in
Suburban Court. Probation was common; 54 percent of Suburban Court youths
(201) received probation for up to two years. Youths could be fined up to
$300, although only 16 (8 percent) were fined as their most severe sanction.
Youths 14 years or older could be sentenced to up to 45 days in the detention
center and youths 18 years or older could be sentenced to up to six months
in the County Jail. These sanctions were used for a few youths: 25 (12 percent)
were sentenced to the Detention Center; 8 (4 percent) were sentenced to the
County Jail.

All these dispositions could be combined with a wide range of terms and
conditions, including restitution, community service, school attendance, re-

strictions on former associations, or participation in drug or family therapy. Youths who violated the terms of their dispositions could be brought back to court for more severe punishment. A revocation of probation was serious because it counted as a new adjudication and thus moved the youth closer to the three adjudications necessary for mandatory placement under a state repeat offender statute, which specified only the number of offenses with no consideration of severity.

A portion of the youths who were adjudicated delinquent were removed from their homes for a maximum period of two years, with the possibility of an extension after judicial review. Twenty-five youths (12 percent) were placed in residential child-care facilities funded by the department of Social Services. An additional 12 youths were committed to the state Department of Institutions (DOI) for a period not to exceed two years, which was usually considered the most severe placement alternative. Youths committed to DOI are evaluated by the state Division of Youth Services and then, depending on their needs, are placed in one of a variety of facilities run by or supervised by the Divison.

Analysis of Pending Cases

Sometimes an examination of cases pending for long periods of time can give some clues about what factors can cause delays. Sixty cases that were initiated in 1980 were still pending at the end of our data collection phase in August 1981. Of the 52 for which information was available, exactly half (26) involved either nonresident youths (20) or youths who had moved without leaving an address (6). Nine involved youths with several petitions or cases pending in more than one jurisdiction. It is interesting that half of the youths whose cases were pending (26) had *never* appeared in the court or had anyone appear for them. The survey of pending cases suggests that high mobility or the commission of offenses outside of one's home jurisdiction are associated both with delay in case processing and with the ultimate lack of case resolution.

Discussion

Suburban Court perceived itself as having a delay problem and clearly it did. Problems were most acute at the beginning of the process. A large portion of the total case time occurred before a youth had his or her advisement hearing, and a substantial amount of it was in the stage between apprehension and the filing of a petition, that is, between the police and the prosecutor, and preceding court involvement. The IJA-ABA Juvenile Standards (1980a) recommend that if a juvenile is not in custody, the prosecutor should file a petition within five days of the time that he or she received the recommendation of the intake officer. But in Suburban Court there was no intake officer and no clearly defined date at which the police responsibility for the case ended and the prosecutor's began.

Why were the case processing times so long in Suburban Court? The answer is not certain, although court employees would probably argue that resources in this particular court system have not kept pace with the rapidly expanding court population and workload. Certainly this was true, yet court resources were increased substantially during the time period under study, with the addition of a second juvenile prosecutor in February, 1980, and of a half-time juvenile judge on January 1, 1981. But even with these additions, both of whom played major roles in handling cases that entered the court in the last half of 1980, the court still had problems processing cases within a reasonable timeframe. Indeed, case processing times continued to climb over the next two years (SYP, 1153).

There is nothing about this court to suggest its cases were unusually complex, and observation over many months showed that court personnel worked conscientiously and consistently to keep up with the caseload. However, at least three handicaps can be identified. The court did not have clearly defined case processing time *goals* that stated standards for handling juvenile cases. It also did not have *leadership* in the effort to reduce case processing time. Was the problem the responsibility of the presiding judge of the district court, the court administrator, or each individual juvenile court judge? Finally, management information was not available. The court essentially dealt with each day's docket as it came up, rather than within the context of a total body of cases. Suburban Court, like many other courts, did not have baseline data—*information* on the existing pace of litigation in the court; the size, age, status of the pending caseload; and the rate at which the court had taken in and disposed of cases in the past (Mahoney B., and Sipes, 1985).

Case processing time is a management problem as well as a legal issue, one that has important implications for the theory of juvenile justice and the role of the court in creating change in troublesome youths. Time as a resource can be used in many ways. But it is not infinitely expandable. Changes in a system cost time while personnel adjust to new ways of doing things and new demands. Time is often a hidden cost of organizational decisions.

We had no way to measure the resource costs of court delay to various parts of the system, but we can speculate about some of them. Appearances that do not further a case cost in court time, staff time, and child time. Given the high turnover in some agencies, like social services and even public defender's and prosecutor's offices, drawn-out cases were often handled by several different staff members. Each one had to take time to learn about the case from the beginning. Youths held in detention for long periods pending a court decision drain resources that yield little positive effects and may cost greatly in terms of child time and intervention time. Long case-processing times reverberate out to the whole court network, adding to already serious resource problems.

5

Constraints on Court Autonomy

Suburban Court faces both economic and legislative constraints, and its operations are dependent to some extent on decision makers who are not necessarily in sympathy with its objectives or perspectives. The court does not control funding for services it orders, for instance, and has only limited ability to influence legislation that dictates the range of its dispositional alternatives. Its operations and its network of services are supported by a complex mix of local, state, federal, and private funds and its actions interface with all levels of government, including municipalities.

This chapter describes the financial structure within which the court works, and traces the development of legislation that ultimately limited the out-of-home placement of children and restructured the financing of services for them. The financial issues and legislative mandates described here create a framework for the court and agency actions discussed in subsequent chapters.

Complex financial and political arrangements among agencies, governmental units, and private parties influence action in the court. When the juvenile court changed from county to a state authority, it gained a greater claim on state resources, while at the same time the community lost some degree of control over its operations. As a result, the control of resources and the locus of real decision-making power were issues that simmered just under the surface of many meetings and discussions relating to Suburban Court.

The state is involved in every level of juvenile court services, and provides funding primarily from three separate sources within state government: The Department of Social Services, which reimburses the county's placement costs on a 80/20 ratio; the Department of Institutions, which runs pretrial detention centers, long-term treatment facilities, and residential mental health institutions; and the Judicial Department, which pays the salaries of court and probation employees, who are housed in county owned and maintained buildings. Each of these state agencies is autonomous, with its own regulations and objectives. Each is subject to its own resource limitations and organizational constraints. And as we will see in this chapter, each influences the services that Suburban Court can provide to individual youths who come into its jurisdiction and the court's ability to adapt to change.

The District Attorney is paid from a combination of state and county sources. In 1980, when Suburban County's District Attorney ran uncontested for reelection for his fourth term, he received 80 percent of his salary from the state and 20 percent from the four counties comprising the judicial district he served. He had to ask the county commissioners for a 29 percent pay raise in order to bring his salary above that of his first assistant, who is paid completely with county funds (SYPN, 91).

Different levels of government have different accounting systems and fiscal years. Suburban County is set up on an accrual system in which funds are reimbursed or advanced by the state on a cash basis. The county's fiscal year runs January 1 to December 31, and the state's runs July 1 to June 30. These differences make county budgeting difficult. For example, the state allotment for the last half of the county's budget year, i.e., from July 1 to December 31, is not known to the county when it prepares its budget in September because the state does not establish its new budget for its July to June fiscal year until the spring (SYP, 1080).

There are other interests in Suburban Court besides state and county governments. The Public Defender's Office, which provides a full-time attorney to Suburban Court, is a statewide organization whose attorneys rotate

through several different offices in different locations as well as from lower   65
to higher courts. (Some private attorneys are also occasionally assigned to
youths, at the expense of the court.) Police officers work for and are paid by
ten different municipalities. County sheriffs provide law enforcement for un-
incorporated areas of the county, but also provide many services for the juvenile court, including the personal delivery of summonses to youths,
transportation of youths to and from the detention center, and provision of
security services. In 1980 a substantial amount of the money for their salaries
was funneled into the county under federal revenue sharing (SYPN, 75).

The funding of mental health services and educational programs is important to the court as well. Mental health centers, whose staff members
sometimes appear in court and to whom many youths are referred, have state,
local, and private components. The state Department of Education also has
some responsibility because of the need for educational services for juveniles
within residential facilities. Such services became a major issue for Suburban
Court during 1980 and 1981, largely because of new federal legislation mandating local funding of special education services to all children who were in
need of them. Interpretation of the new legislation was the subject of heated
debate, in part because of contradictions between different statutes, but also
because local school districts, already suffering from rapid and uneven expansion, were particularly concerned about who would shoulder the financial
burden for educational services in county programs for court youths.

The federal government's financial presence in Suburban Court is less
obvious than the state's, but is relevant none the less. The District Attorney's
Diversion Program, supported in 1980 with 75 percent state funds and 25
percent local funds, started out as a federally funded experimental program
supported by the Law Enforcement Assistance Administration. Two new
programs started by the state in Suburban Court in 1980 were demonstration
programs supported by federal funds awarded to the state and allocated by
the state to Suburban County. In addition, roughly 60 percent of the state's
reimbursement to the county for placement costs came from federal appropriations to the state.

The cost of juvenile court services is not just carried by public agencies.
Families of children in court pay too, and are assessed on a needs basis for the
cost of their child's treatment. In 1980 this was becoming an increasingly
important part of the total financing of juvenile services, and every family met
with a social worker to establish a formula for family contribution to treatment,
which was included in the court order for placement (SYP, 387). Social service
workers told us that close to 100 percent of the families were ordered to pay
some portion of the cost of services (SYP, 994–995). Families who fell behind

in payments could be taken to court by the department of social services (SYP, 387).

Social Services—The Key to Treatment Facilities

The county department of social services, through its foster care budget, controls and pays for most of Suburban Court's pretrial and residential treatment programs except for those programs involving the small number of youths who are committed to the state Department of Institutions. The budget comes from a cumbersome combination of local, state, and federal levels of government, with its largest share coming from state reimbursement of 80 percent of placement costs up to a maximum amount of net reimbursable expenditures. Until 1980, state allocations and budgets for placement continued to expand, (SYP, 1081) until the financial situation changed on the national scene as well as on local and state levels. At that time, the county department of social services found itself financially squeezed by both the county and the state.

County Resources

The foster care budget of social services, which comes from Suburban County's Welfare Fund, is the largest single fund in the county aside from the county General Fund (SYP, 1074). This fund is allocated by the county commissioners and came to be viewed with trepidation by them and by other officials in this fiscally and politically conservative area. In spite of its rapidly growing population and the need for more services, the county had been able to avoid tax rate increases for several years, mainly because the rapid rise of property valuation in the county had added to property tax revenues. Prior to 1980, in fact, the county had been able to carry over substantial amounts of money from one fiscal year to the next (SYPN, 97), and was unprepared for the harsher economic realities of the 1980s.

In 1980 the financial situation in the county at last necessitated serious discussion about the need to raise taxes. Hoping to avoid such increases, the commissioners scrutinized the budget sharply and developed it with "the objective of limiting expenditures, while continuing the efficient delivery of county services" (SYP, 1077). In pursuit of this objective, requests for new personnel and/or programs were denied except in special circumstances. Cost-of-living increases for county employees were limited to 7 percent and budget requests from all departments were studied more carefully.

County officials kept the increase of the total 1980 county budget to 8.7 percent over the 1979 budget, with an 11% increase in the Welfare Fund (SYP, 1077). In addition, they utilized budget surpluses that had previously carried over to the next year to fund some supplemental appropriations approved by the county commissioners, including two in law enforcement—new employees for the county sheriff's department and money to complete a new jail addition. But despite these measures, fiscal experts predicted a carry-over of only $200,000 from 1980 to 1981 and argued that in 1981 the county commissioners would have to either raise property taxes or reduce departmental budgets (SYPN, 97). They did both, and a prime target of the 1981 budget cuts was the large Welfare Fund, which had grown 2.3 percent more than the budget as a whole in 1980. The unwillingness of the county commissioners to indefinitely raise the budget for social services became obvious as they slashed social services requests by one million dollars. Most of the money, $750,000, came from aid to dependent children. The rest came from the foster care program, from which most court ordered services were supported (SYPN, 179).

State Resources

Up until fiscal year 1979–80, fiscal cooperation between the state and county provided a good hedge for the county against rapidly rising placement costs. The state had essentially provided a blank check to the county, with 80 percent reimbursement of county placement costs and yearly allocations that were based on the prior year's expenditures. As the county's placement costs had gone up, so had the state's allocation to the county social services. When the county went beyond its allocation, the state covered the difference with a supplemental allocation.

Under this arrangement, costs rose rapidly. In 1977, Suburban County was allotted $808,940 and spent $927,500; in 1978 it was allotted $1,037,919 and spent $1,458,400; in 1979 it was allotted $1,500,000 and spent $2,172,000. In 1980, for the first time, the county was allocated less than it had spent the previous year, only $2,000,000 (SYP, 1080), although it spent even more, $2,414,717. In 1980–81, supplements and ever-increasing allotments for the future came to an abrupt end. Like other state agencies, the State Department of Social Services was held to an annual budget increase of 7 percent, and had become concerned with rapidly spiraling placement costs, raging far above the 7 percent ceiling.

The new law to limit out-of-home placement that went into effect in January 1980 was heralded as the answer to expanding costs. In October 1980 as part of the implementation of the bill, the state adopted an allocation methodology to be phased in over a six-year period. Under the new plan, allocations would be based decreasingly on previous expenditures for foster care. Future allocations would be calculated on a formula based on indicators of social disruption and need for social services in each county. During the first year (fiscal year 1979–1980) allocations were to be based only on prior year expenditures, as they had been in the past. In the second year, the new formula would begin to go into effect. Over five years the state allocations would become increasingly based on current needs rather than past expenditures (SYP, 826). But Suburban County had grown highly dependent on annual increases in state allocations and probably would not fare as well financially under the new formula. Compared to many other counties in the state, it had substantial resources and was not likely to be a top candidate for state allocations on the basis of "social disruption and need for social services."

Social Services Limit Residential Placements

As state and local administrators struggled to bring rising costs down to meet shrinking resources, they began to exert more overt financial constraints on court decision makers. Although the court's ideology continued to reflect the "best interest of the child," the county director of social services was facing a shortfall of $185,000 (SYP, 851), and measures had to be taken. Finally, in late April, 1981, he circulated a memo to supervisors, social services staff, and other agencies, notifying them that under a 1973 state legislative mandate that put a ceiling on expenditures for child placements, there would be no additional residential placements until there was a significant decrease in the number of children placed (SYP, 885).

The memo raised questions about decision-making power in juvenile court. In a meeting called in response to the memo by an interagency policy group concerned with alternatives to placement, members asked whether financial constraints could override judicial decisions. If they cannot, members asked, where does the money come from to pay for court-ordered placements? Agency workers asked the director of social services if the juvenile judge ordered placement of a child, which agency and which decision would prevail?

"Judges don't understand budgets and don't feel budget problems," the director responded (SYP, 856).

Social services apparently chose to sidestep a direct confrontation on the issue, but informal attempts were made to sensitize the judge to budget problems. Several county commissioners reportedly visited him to ask his help in reducing placements and alleviating the financial crisis, but the judge was

reportedly not sympathetic to elevating the importance of cost in his decision
making, and responded that his duty was to act in the best interest of the child
(SYP, 991). Furthermore, he articulated this view directly in a July 1981 interview in which he expressed concern about the unwillingness of social services to make placements, and reiterated his belief that the lack of placement
was hurting individual children. He also added that recently he had been
ordering social services to place children out of the home and that so far there
had been no refusals (SYP, 956).

Financial pressures on the decisions of participants in the juvenile justice
network became more acute as the court was squeezed between state and
county cost cutters and ever-expanding client populations. Financial pressure
pervaded the juvenile justice system, and dreams and dollars came into direct
competition as the judge's continued advocacy of the "best interest of the
child" was viewed with increasing annoyance by some county officials.

In spite of the judge's overt refusal to make crucial decisions on the basis
of cost, *somebody* was. As 1980 moved into 1981, the number of children in
placement dropped, rather than increasing at the rate of 5.5 percent per quarter
as the county director of social services had projected it would. In January
1980 there were 355 youths in placement; by May there were only 305; and
by March 1981 there were only 266.

Suburban Court pinned its hopes for cost reduction in large part on
programs developed through and paid for by start-up funds tied to the legislation to reduce out-of-home placement. (Start-up funds were monies set
aside to help counties begin new programs, but they were allocated with the
idea that some influx of new money was necessary to help counties through
the transitional period before their new programs showed a cost reduction and
could thus be self-supporting.) The legislation that went into effect in January
1980 had a strong ideological dimension, and it was hailed by child advocates
as an important reform—an integral part of the larger national trend toward
deinstitutionalization and diversion. But its passage and implementation also
raise many issues about the complex dilemma of attaining goals with limited
resources.

A Legislative Attempt to Reduce Out-of-Home Placement

Legislation to reduce out-of-home placement of children was passed in the last
few minutes of the 1979 state legislative session—the result of a coalition
between child welfare advocates, children's rights supporters, and conservative
legislators. The child advocates sought to protect children from getting "lost"

in placement and from unnecessary state intervention in their lives. The conservatives hoped to reduce the alarmingly rapid rise of placement costs. This alliance between conservatives and child advocates symbolizes much of the tension within the juvenile justice system in general and sets the scene for many of the local controversies that accompanied the implementation of the bill in its first year.

On the surface, the legislation appeared to be an expression of the national trend toward an expansion of children's rights, because the reduction of out-of-home placement minimizes state intervention in the lives of children. However, if we analyze it in more depth using Teilmann and Klein's conceptual scheme for predicting and assessing the acceptance of a new legislation, we get a broader view (1980). They describe the legislation in terms of three concepts—signals, reflections, and control.

The *signals* of a new piece of legislation to anticipated audiences, in this case the practitioners in the juvenile justice network and the budget makers, include clarity of legislative intent, legislative mandate, and fiscal implications. The intent to use the least restrictive placement possible for a child appeared clear until practitioners began to question whether "least restrictive" was necessarily synonymous with "the best interest" of the child. One of the strongest signals the legislation sent out, which became increasingly obvious over the first year of implementation, had to do with the fiscal implications of the bill. Cost reduction was seen as an important part of the legislation.

The new legislation *reflected* several state and national trends: a growing concern for children's rights, movement toward deinstitutionalization, and reduction of governmental expenditures for human services. These trends are somewhat contradictory in their practical implications, so that practitioners responded to them differently in different situations.

The *control* dimension of this legislation primarily involved a balance of state and local control over services and resources, and some potential reallocation of power between the judicial system and social services. These dimensions will be discussed in more detail in the rest of this chapter.

Suburban County moved quickly to implement the legislation. Before discussing the county's programs and efforts to implement the legislation in Chapters 6 and 7, it is useful to get some background on the bill itself—its history, intent, mechanisms for implementation, and issues.

History—The 1978 Study of Out-of-Home Placement

As a result of widespread dissatisfaction with the state's out-of-home placement programs in all three branches of government, the State Legislature in 1978 authorized an Out-of-Home Placement Study by the Office of Planning and 71 Budgeting. The findings of the study provided the basis for the bill endorsed at the 1979 legislative session.

One of the most important findings of the study was that out-of-home placement costs represented one of the fastest growing components of the state budget, an increase from 9 million dollars in 1973–74 to an estimated 30 million dollars in 1979–80. The average cost of placement and the number of placements increased 140% and 38% (SYP, 1151.3). Both exceeded the rate of increase in prices generally or the population growth in the state. The study suggested that agency workers were using placement more frequently as a primary response to the problems of a difficult child rather than as a treatment option of last resort (SYP, 1151.4). Some of the reasons for this articulated in the study include organizational problems, financial factors, and lack of judicial review of placements.

Organizational Problems   One set of reasons involved organizational arrangements—lack of coordinated planning for children due to lack of clear definition of agency roles at both the state and local levels. Lack of clear responsibility and criteria for placement resulted in placement policies that differed by agency and geographic area. The problems were made more acute by insufficient information—it was not possible to track children over the full course of their treatment to assess their needs or program effectiveness.

Another organizational factor of central importance was the lack of non-residential treatment options. Often a child could get necessary treatment *only* in a residential setting, even though the child did not otherwise need to be taken out of his or her home. There was also a growing belief that some children could get the treatment they needed only outside the state: in November 1979, 139 children were in out-of-state placement, most ordered into specific programs by judges because they felt state resources were not available to meet the needs of individual children (SYP, 830).[1]

Financial Structure   Financial factors actually encouraged out-of-home placement. Much of the money allocated to counties for children's services could be used *only* for residential services.[2] Furthermore, the rates of some kinds of service provided were not responsive to changing conditions. Thus, some family foster homes and group homes (representing the least restrictive as well as the less expensive side of the continuum of residential care), went out of business because their rates were not cost-based, e.g. they were not based on the cost of providing services, food, etc., to the children in their care, and did not rise with costs. Rates of the more restrictive residential child-care facilities were cost-based and were adjusted upwards as necessary.

A variation on this problem was the financial incentive that state cost restrictions gave courts to place youths outside the state. The state legislature in 1979 set a limit of $1,812 per month per child placed in-state, but permitted $2,135 per month for children placed outside the state. The higher rates ostensibly permitted better treatment facilities and the only way to get these superior services for children was to send them across state borders. The rate limitation eliminated the use of one highly regarded local placement because of its cost, but enabled courts to use the same organization's similarly priced facilities in nearby states.

Another concern was that some decision makers, to keep their own costs down, would seek out what appeared to be "free" placements paid for by other agencies rather than the most appropriate placement for the child. The referral of children to hospitals by county social service workers, for example, shifted the cost of care from the county social service budget to the state Department of Institutions. On the other side, transfer of youths from facilities run by the state's Department of Institutions to local group homes or residential child-care facilities could shift costs from the state back to the county.

Concern about educational costs surfaced in the report at the same time it became an issue elsewhere in the system and nationally. The report argued that education costs should not be included as part of placement expense because a child receives education whether he or she is in placement or the community, and that educational cost should come from the child's own school district.

Review of Placements The study of out-of-home placement also identified as a problem the lack of procedures for judicial review of some kinds of placements, especially voluntary ones. Although the Children's Code provided for review of the continued need of adjudicated youths to remain in placement, there had been no legislation requiring review of cases of *all* children placed outside the home. In fact, the study identified a sizable number of children who had been in placement for years without any reevaluation of their need for placement or their response to it.

The problems identified in the Out-of-Home Placement Study, especially the importance of financial and organizational structures in promoting certain kinds of programs, provided fairly accurate predictions about the areas in which problems developed implementating the bill. Although it remained unarticulated, the underlying purpose of the bill was not just to reduce out-of-home placement but to modify the whole fabric of child-care services in the state.

The legislation's intent was to control the increasing costs of out-of-home placements of delinquent and nondelinquent children and to limit the number and duration of such placements, thus minimizing state intervention in the lives of children. Jurisdiction was given to juvenile courts to review any out-of-home placement of a child that exceeded or was expected to exceed 90 days and for regular review of placements every six months thereafter. The court had to decide by a preponderance of the evidence obtained from an evaluation of the child whether or not placement or continued placement was necessary and was in the best interest of the child and the community. If placements were made, they had to be for a determinate period and had to be reviewed regularly by the court.

One of the most important aspects of the bill was the increased flexibility and control it gave to local communities in regard to children's services, by encouraging them to develop programs that provided services to children who remained in their own homes. Formerly, allocations to counties for services could be used *only* to pay the costs of a child's out-of-home placement. Under the new bill, these allocations could be used for a wide range of services if the county established a placement alternatives commission and if they could be shown to reduce the number, duration, intensity, or distance from home of out-of-home placements.

Mechanics of Implementation

The initial plans for implementation of the bill involved the establishment of a Placement Alternatives Commission (PAC) in each county composed of community representatives and the directors of agencies involved with juveniles. The PAC was required to develop a plan for the reduction of out-of-home placement of children in its community. A start-up fund of $500,000 of state money was set aside for the first year and a county could apply for a share of the money once it had developed a plan. Although the amount of start-up funds was small, it was hoped that the money would be an important incentive. Without it, counties with their foster care funds fully committed to existing children and programs would not have the financial latitude to develop new programs. It was anticipated that once a program that kept children at home got underway, it would be able to pay for itself as a result of the savings generated through a decrease in out-of-home placement costs. At the same time, of course, this approach put pressure on new programs to show immediate financial benefits.

Several mechanisms were set up to help the implementation of the legislation. One was the development of specific criteria for placement. A second was a staff development project funded under a one-year federal grant that helped communities develop plans for alternatives to out-of-home placement and disseminated information and training materials on community treatment programs.

A third mechanism was the Coalition Regarding Child Placement, a voluntary association composed of the League of Women Voters, Metropolitan Child Protection Council, Junior League, and National Council of Jewish Women. The purpose of the coalition was to monitor the implementation of the bill and to encourage the most constructive application of its provisions (SYP, 1152).

There were many practical problems of implementation that arose from the issues raised by the legislation and the different interests to which it resonated. Part of the task of implementation in the early months was to identify the trouble spots in the law and mark them for amendment in the 1981 legislative session.

Issues Raised by Legislation

The law raised several important issues that would continue to trouble concerned citizens and officials throughout the state in the 1980–81 period. Some of the issues were political and philosophical; others were practical problems involved in making any new piece of legislation compatible with related state, local, and federal statutes and regulations.

Is Least Restrictive Always in the Child's Best Interest?

As we have already seen, an important philosophical theme that underlies much of the discussion surrounding the legislation is the tension between cutting costs and the obligation to provide children with the most extensive programs possible. During the first two years of implementation, conservative legislation and other budget-conscious supporters of the law were eager to see benefits in terms of reduced foster care budgets at the local level. To them, the law legitimated the reduction of out-of-home placement costs and mandated the use of less expensive services. Child advocates, on the other hand, were eager to keep children out of placement and see innovations effected in services, but worried that over-eagerness to show short-term cost reductions could set programs and youths up for long-term failure. They feared, moreover, that new community programs, under pressure to reach capacity and show cost savings, might not be able to give sufficient attention to the selection of the most appropriate youths for the program and the best mix of youths for an effective treatment environment.

Widening the Intervention Net

A second issue, which has been discussed at length in regard to other deinstitutionalization programs (e.g., Klein, 1984; Vinter, Downs, and Hall, 1975), is whether an emphasis on in-home services simply widens the intervention net. If staff members bring into community programs youths who would not previously have been placed in treatment programs, might they be expanding rather than narrowing the service network, with a resulting increase, at least in the short range, in juvenile service budgets? This possibility seems less likely in the implementation of this law than in other deinstitutionalization programs because of the strong emphasis on cost reduction and fairly stringent evaluation requirements.

As time went on, this possibility became even less of a concern. This is notable given the prevalence of net widening in earlier deinstitutionalization programs. It may be that "net widening" is only a problem in times of affluence. In 1980, funds available for placement were not only not expanding as they had been before, they were not even keeping up with the need for placement. There were few resources available to support the widening of treatment populations.

Balance of State and Local Power

A third issue with high political and financial salience involves the balance between local and state control. In some ways, the new legislation gave more autonomy to local communities because it enabled them to use allocations more flexibly to fund community treatment programs designed specifically to meet their own needs. On the other hand, it extended state control since it required state approval of a county plan, which had to be updated yearly, and involved extensive data collection, evaluation procedures, and financial arrangements.

Some counties were better able to take advantage of the state resources than others. Suburban Court, for example, with its large population base and already existing interagency network, geared itself up immediately to request a third of the total first year start-up funds. Other counties with less resources moved more slowly and may have felt the limitations on their autonomy more keenly than the new benefits.

A fourth issue raised by the law involved the autonomy of local juvenile court judges. One of the main drafters of the bill had sought to eliminate judicial discretion altogether in regard to specific placements for individual children, but this had been resisted by both juvenile court judges and district attorneys. The final version of the bill decreased, but did not eliminate, judicial discretion in regard to placement. It did, however, limit the placement power of local juvenile court judges in regard to out-of-state placements by giving the power of review of these placement decisions to state-level officials. This part of the legislation substantially increased the power of state administrative authorities over local decision makers. Like other parts of the law, it raised some interesting questions about the respective power of state and local officials as well as judicial and administrative decision makers.

Feasibility of Court Review of Placement

A fifth issue was whether court review of placement was an appropriate device for the monitoring of children already in placement, and whether the process could be handled effectively by courts without any increase in resources. Although adjudicated youths had had placement reviews prior to the legislation, they had not had them as frequently as the new legislation required, and some categories of children in placement had not had any reviews at all. Officials throughout the state worried that the 90-day reviews and subsequent six-month reviews of all placements would add hundreds of hearings each year to already overcrowded dockets. At least one juvenile court judge resigned, citing, among other reasons, fear of work overload as a result of the reviews required by the legislation. Another estimated that as a result of the new requirement, her jurisdiction would have to conduct at least 1,442 new reviews (SYPN, 134).

In addition to the actual review of placements, courts anticipated that they also would be responsible for issuing summonses for each review and preparing detailed reports to justify any placement of any child in an out-of-state facility, all additions to already heavy workloads. The Judicial Department had added a fiscal note to the bill when it was being considered, indicating that a state appropriation of $800,000 would be necessary to take care of its first year impact on the state's courts, but the bill was approved without the funding.

Without any additional resources, then, the additional reviews threatened to clog the court to the extent that children charged with offenses or awaiting

disposition might have to wait even longer before their cases could be resolved. 77
Furthermore, there was considerable confusion about when the first review had to be done and whether the reviews could be record reviews by the judge or required the presence of all interested parties in the court room.

Potential Problems of Implementation

The legislation to limit out-of-home placement of children stirred up the juvenile justice system throughout the state and threw into question a set of previous assumptions about how the system worked and how agencies interacted with one another. In some important ways, the law shifted control to local communities with its assumption that local planners knew what would work in their communities. On the other hand, state requirements for yearly plans and evaluations kept close reins on local court systems. The legislation, as it moved into its implementation stage, held at least the potential for changes in the structure of power relations between agencies and levels of government.

Studies suggest that implementation is a political process and that a key factor in its success is the motivation of practitioners (Baum, 1976; Van Horn and Van Meter, 1977). The out-of-home-placement law needed the support of a wide variety of practitioners at different points in the juvenile justice network. Would it be able to garner that support? Several aspects of the legislation made widespread agreement about its desirability unlikely.

Change and cost are interwoven. Changes in resource availability often create chaos in organizational networks and treatment priorities. An expansion of resources may bring new programs, more flexibility, and an interest in bringing in more clients. Reduction of resources, as in this instance, may bring an emphasis on gate keeping activities to curtail intake, restructure priorities, and protect agencies and individuals from overwork and overextension (Lawson and Gletne, 1982). It may also lead to more joint programs and more interdependent relationships (Aiken and Hage, 1968). The new law then became both a vehicle and a scapegoat. Logically the new legislation refined the concept of "best interest" to include the notion of "least restrictive placement," a position compatible with the beliefs of most advocates of children's rights. Although this would seem to clarify the juvenile court's goals and provide a more precise basis for selecting among alternatives in making a disposition decision, the concept was no easier to define than the concept of "best interest of the child." In assuming that children were always better off at home unless they were in danger or a threat to themselves or others, did the law limit consideration of other needs like the need for nurturance or opportunity for optimal growth and development?

The law, passed at a time when cost reduction was becoming a high priority at all levels of the public sector, legitimated efforts to limit cost by reducing placement. It also legitimated the overt discussion of cost as a factor in decisions about individual children, effectively shifting it upward in ranking. As the next chapter shows, many individuals and agencies felt uncomfortable with this shift.

6

Negotiations for Change and Resources

The Placement Alternatives Commission

The law to reduce out-of-home placement became a significant factor in Suburban Court's environment, and negotiations about its effect started between the court network and state authorities and among agencies within the network almost from the moment of its passage. Actually, the legislation had a formal mechanism for these negotiations built into it, a requirement for a Placement Alternatives Commission (PAC) in each court jurisdiction. This Commission was designed to be an interagency policy-making group composed of administrators from each court's public child-serving agencies as well as a community representative.

One of the goals of the Placement Alternatives Commission in Suburban County was to open channels of communication among agencies. At the same time, it was to provide a means for members of the court network to articulate network goals, identify areas especially affected by the new laws, and renegotiate procedures and funding priorities, as well as negotiate for resources (Drabek and Chapman, 1973).

Legislated change does not just fall into place once a law is passed. Sometimes laws do not have their desired effect (Macaulay, 1979) or produce effects other than what was anticipated (Croyle, 1979). The impact of a change is negotiated at the environmental, intermediate, and individual levels of organizational systems. Successful implementation of an innovation depends for example, on how much adjustment in procedures and work group norms it demands (Emrick and Peterson, 1978; and Smith & Keith, 1971) and the level of resources it requires. New programs that are perceived as adding new work without increasing rewards are likely to be resisted (Scheirer, 1981:48).

The new legislation and its accompanying programs disrupted the power relationships that had been in effect in Suburban Court and between the court and state agencies. Previously, systems had been organized vertically. The new legislation, which attempted to develop a partnership between state and local agencies, attempted to move toward horizontal structures. This attempted shift was not often articulated and probably was generally unrecognized, although it was talked about by a few people at the state level (SYP, 1153).

This major change provided a structure to allow local communities to develop programs of their own that they were responsible for and could be integrated within the community. By removing restrictions on the kinds of treatment facilities the state would help fund, and by encouraging local communities to develop programs especially suited to their needs, the new legislation expanded the potential for innovation in the treatment of troubled children. The PAC was the arena in which these innovations could develop and in which relationships among agencies could be renegotiated.

The personalities in Suburban Court are unique; the battles are specific to them and to a particular period of time and set of issues. But the negotiations over power, turf, money, and ideologies described here illustrate how individuals and organizations in many places attempt to cope with change. They show how organizational subunits may try to promote their own self-interest unless constrained by a clearly defined goal structure (Jones 1982; Perrow 1982:687; Scott 1981). Individuals and groups will influence organizations to the extent that they can; and to the extent that they do, they will push for actions that work to their own personal and organizational advantage unless they are constrained by other individuals, groups, or structures.

The PAC

The PAC of Suburban County was organized almost immediately after the new legislation was passed in July 1979 and was well established when the

legislation went into effect six months later. It immediately assumed a major   81
policy-making role for the court, in that it became responsible for developing
the annual plan for reduction of out-of-home placement now required of all
jurisdictions and became the decision-making and coordination body for all
new programs related to the legislation. Issues surfaced in PAC meetings that
were not clearly articulated anywhere else, and most events concerning juvenile
services eventually came to its attention.

The Commission met weekly in open meetings during its first year and
a half and bi-weekly thereafter. Its official membership included the director
of the youth detention center, the supervisor of juvenile probation, a representative of the bar, the district attorney, the director of community services
for the state division of youth services, the executive directors of the two
mental health centers in the county, the director of the tri-county health department, the chief probation officer, the executive director of a community
training and services center, the director of social services, a community representative, and two representatives of educational systems in the county.

Twelve of the fourteen members attended regularly, along with a few
other nonvoting participants who held key positions in youth-serving agencies
or joined the group as they became directors of new programs. The district
attorney's office rarely sent a representative in the early months, and there was
no representative from the private bar or the public defender's office. Since
some of the regular participants were not official members and some of the
official members rarely attended, there was some confusion about who the
voting members of the group were. This became an issue when the vote was
very close.

The County Plan

Much of the PAC's energy centered initially on developing a county plan for
alternatives to out-of-home placement. Only eleven days after the legislation
went into effect, it submitted its proposal and requested a substantial portion
of the state's total $500,000 start-up funds (SYP, 117–118).

The county plan included three components: the interdisciplinary youth
diagnostic team (referred to generally as the "Team"); two day resource centers; and a "home quest program," designed to retrieve 16 county youths who
had been placed in out-of-state residential facilities. (One other new program,
the detention alternatives program, was not included in the plan since it addressed pretrial detention rather than long-term placement and technically was
not covered by the new legislation. Nevertheless, PAC members considered

it to be within the spirit of the law and thought of it as part of the county's program to reduce out-of-home placement.) The first two components of the proposed plan became central to the county's juvenile court network during the first year of implementation; the third had relatively little impact on the day-to-day activities of the court network and will not be discussed in any detail here.

The diagnostic team and the day resource centers involved complicated reallocations of both power and resources among state and county agencies. The diagnostic team had been planned by the state, independent of and prior to the legislation to limit out-of-home placement. It combined federal, state, and local financing. The state had already been awarded federal funds which it had decided to split between the team and the detention alternatives project in Suburban County. These federal funds paid the salary of a half-time team leader and a secretary. The plan requested state start-up funds to support a case worker and an educational diagnostician and committed county resources from local agencies for two part-time psychologists from the mental health centers, and a nurse from the health center. The Team was responsible for providing full evaluations on all youths age 12 to 18 who were being considered for out-of-home placement.

The county expected to finance the two new day resource centers almost entirely from state start-up funds. The centers, one on the east side of the county and one on the west, were designed to provide nonresidential treatment and education for youths who otherwise would have to be placed outside the home. The detention alternatives program, although not officially in the county plan, was very much intermeshed with other programs and agencies. Operated by the state with federal funds, the program operated out of the local youth detention center, a facility owned by the county. The program's half-time coordinator was scheduled to spend the other half of his time acting as leader for the diagnostic team. The objective of the detention alternatives program was to reduce the number of children who were held in the detention center, which had been chronically overcrowded for years. The project was a high priority item on the PAC's agenda.

PAC Atmosphere

The atmosphere of PAC meetings usually was outwardly relaxed and cordial. Members sold each other their children's Girl Scout cookies and PTA candy, brought each other coffee, and chatted about their golf holidays, and noontime squash games (SYP, 84–85). References were made often to the importance of the Commission and being able to talk together about the issues. Meetings clearly had important symbolic value. The surface congeniality, however, did not overshadow the more serious underlying issues. Although technically the group did not have a chair and members took turns signing for PAC on county plans and other documents, in reality the director of social services chaired the meeting and prepared the agenda. The power this informal leadership entailed was considerable and underlined the control he held over the county's child-care budget. It was not lost on any of the group's members.

The director of social services had been in position for a long time and was generally regarded as having a close relationship with the county commissioners (SYP, 993). More importantly, the director held the purse strings on all funds for out-of-home placement (except for youths committed to the State Department of Institutions) and jealously guarded this power and purse. But although responsible for paying bills and balancing the budget, the director did not have exclusive control over placement decisions. As he put it, "I've got money in checking accounts and the judge has the checks" (SYP, 836). While resources had continued to expand, this separation between resources and decisions was not a problem; when the local social services department used up its allotted funds, the state came to its rescue with a supplemental grant. But the new legislation had changed that, and social services was feeling a growing pressure to keep its costs down and within its own control.

Members of the PAC, along with the judge, also posed problems for the social services budget. Several wanted PAC to take an innovative role in developing new programs (SYP, 544) and saw themselves as responsible for the best interests of children without concern about costs. There was an implicit attitude that if money was needed for children's services, someone, presumably the department of social services or the state, should find it. The "more services, more money" philosophy continued to be espoused by some members of PAC, and the director of social services undoubtedly saw PAC as a potential threat to both his decision-making power and his budget.

Themes Underlying PAC Meetings

Several themes dominated PAC meetings, including the desire for local control, local power conflicts, and disagreement over the meaning of the best interest of the child.

The new legislation narrowed the power of local jurisdictions in some important ways, specifically in requiring a plan for the reduction of out-of-home placement and in giving the final authority for out-of-state placement to the *state* director of social services. Local administrators chafed under these restrictions and vented their frustrations in PAC meetings.

State-local conflict and discussions about state action or the lack of it was a point around which all members of the PAC could coalesce. For example, there were regular expressions of annoyance and anger over the lack of clear state directives for evaluation requirements, data needs, and financial arrangements. One PAC member even refused to consider one of the state's requests. "When they finally make up their minds about what information they want us to collect, we'll make plans to collect it," he exclaimed. "But it doesn't make any sense to start collecting it now. If we do, they will call and tell us they want one more piece and then we'll have to go back and start all over again" (SYP, 204).

There was also ongoing conflict with the state over financing of programs. "The state program people tell me one thing and then the state budget people tell me something completely different," complained one PAC member (SYP, 246). "I don't know where we stand."

The director of social services at one point implied to PAC that the study on which the new legislation had been based was not well thought out. He also indicated that the state department of social services, which administered the implementation of the legislation, was "run" by people from an adjoining and rival county (SYP, 504). Tension then was not just between the county and the state, but between counties as well.

The state's new power to veto out-of-state placement was seen as a serious infringement of local authority, and with the approval of PAC members, Suburban County was quick to respond. On January 4, when the juvenile judge ordered a boy to placement in an adjacent state, officials from the facility, who were in the courtroom, could not act because state officials had not signed the necessary papers. Angered, the judge announced to a courtroom packed with local court officials and agency staff members that if the state did not act by January 7 at 1:30 P.M., he would issue a contempt citation to the state official holding up the placement. "We probably could have sold tickets to this hearing," said one probation officer (SYP, 6).

Finally, on January 8 the documents were signed. The boy was packed and ready to go, but this time there was no representative to take him, so the judge had no choice but to order one more night in the detention center. While

social services made arrangements for a plane ticket, the boy appeared dis-
tressed. "I don't want to stay there, even one more night," he told the judge.
The boy had been waiting more than a year for a final resolution of his case
(SYP, 13).

Battle lines were drawn more firmly by March, when a second out-of-
state placement became an issue. At that time, Suburban County's diagnostic
team evaluated a child held in detention and recommended an out-of-state
placement which was approved by the county social services department. The
judge agreed with the recommendation. The case entailed a 15-year-old ha-
bitual runaway who had been in and out of hearings and placements in two
counties for three years. In the past he had set fire to a house and attacked a
boy with a knife, although he was not currently before the court on a delinquency charge, and was not thought to be certifiable as mentally ill or mentally
deficient. The diagnostic team and others working with him believed that the
best program, and in fact the only one available that offered any hope of
success, was one located outside the state. The placement would cost roughly
$3,000 a month for an anticipated three years (SYP, 356).

Under its new authority, the state vetoed the placement and refused to
pay its 80% share, asserting that the boy could be treated appropriately in an
adolescent treatment unit of the state mental hospital. Advocates for the youth,
including the director of the local mental health center, argued that the local
program was not adequate because the boy needed longer treatment than the
program's maximum six months and because he was not mentally ill. During
the controversy the boy waited in the youth detention center for over 100
days without treatment, essentially between the cracks of service agencies
(SYPN, 100). The case was followed closely by workers in Suburban County
and weekly reports were given on its status in PAC meetings. It was one of
the few issues on which everyone in PAC agreed; the state was clearly the
enemy and locals were united against it (SYP, 353).

The child was finally ordered to the out-of-state facility by the judge in
May and departed in early June with the necessary papers signed. The controversy over who would ultimately pay for the placement still raged. In late
June, the state sent a letter to Suburban County's department of social services
stating that it would *not* pay the 80% reimbursement. In August, the Guardian
Ad Litem appointed for the youth by the judge asked the court to order the
state department of social services to pay 80% of the cost (SYPN, 100), which
the judge did the following month. In his ruling, he called the state action "an
insensitive sabotage of a court order," and suggested that neither the state
director of social services nor the state department of social services has an
"appellate power" to overrule or countermand a judge's ruling. If they did,

all the "good work" done by crisis teams, social workers, and others who make recommendations to the courts about child placement in dependency and neglect actions "would be subject to the director's review" (SYPN, 128). The State Attorney General's office contended, on the other hand, that the judge did not have the jurisdiction to order payment, and that the question was an internal matter between state and county departments of social services.

This case illustrates how cost, legislation, protection of turf, and decisions about a child's best interest interweave to create controversy and restrict the court's ability to act in a timely manner to meet a child's needs. Some states confer statutory authority on juvenile courts to compel, by writ of mandamus, the appropriation of any funds necessary for the operation of the court. This power is frequently held to include appropriations for such services as probation, intake, detention, foster care, and counseling. When budget requests are denied, judges have sometimes resorted to invoking this power, occasionally jailing officials for contempt (Pettibone, 1981:382). The human cost of ongoing battles over services is important too. In this instance, a disturbed adolescent was stored in a secure detention facility for two months *after* a decision about his treatment had been made, while state and local officials argued about who would pay for it.

Local Power Conflicts

Questions of local power relationships were very much on the agenda in the PAC, but rarely articulated. There was a general unease about how the new programs and procedures might modify the existing balance of power and the territorial prerogatives of county juvenile agencies and workers. It was difficult to follow these conflicts, moreover, since a great deal of the discussion and the actual decision making took place in hallways, offices, and over the telephone. On several occasions, a PAC meeting was adjourned with matters tending toward one direction or completely unresolved. At the next meeting, it would become clear that a decision had already been made. Sometimes the drift of the decision-making process would reverse and the actions ultimately taken would be quite different from those an outsider might have predicted on the basis of the previous meeting's discussions.

One clear-cut example of PAC's internal power struggles surrounds the decision about whom to hire as the group's administrator. At first the decision seemed simple enough, but it soon evolved into an emotionally charged issue. The stakes were high, and the outcome of the conflict involved control of the group and the direction in which the group would move.

In late January the state responded to the County's plan, asked for an

addendum, and recommended that PAC hire an administrator to do its staff   87
work. Up to that point work for PAC had been carried out primarily by the
department of social services (SYP, 84). Discussion about the organizational
role of the administrator started January 30 and continued for several weeks
(SYP, 84). One member of PAC suggested that the administrator could work
for the diagnostic team leader who had just been hired. Another suggested
that the team leader should work for the administrator. It was equally unclear
how the administrator would relate to the coordinators of the day resource
centers, who had not yet been selected (SYP, 102). One of the probation
officers suggested that the administrator should organize PAC priorities, set
agendas, keep a history of the commission, and manage its tasks—in other
words, take over most of the work presently being handled by the director
of social services.

In the addendum to the county plan prepared by PAC the staff administrator was described as someone who would be "responsible for administration, coordination, and evaluation of all PAC programs including the East
and West Day Resource Centers, monitoring the Home Quest Program, development and administration of such future PAC programs as preventive
programs for children ages 0 to 12 and emancipation programs for youths 17
and over." The salary was set at $20,000 (SYP, 93–95).

The topic of the PAC administrator became more emotional as the weeks
wore on. The young, capable supervisor of the adolescent program in social
services had been doing a great deal of extra work for the PAC, and some
speculated—outside the meetings—that he would be a good candidate. When
it was suggested that a job description be prepared for the February 20 meeting,
the adolescent program supervisor volunteered to write it. His description
very carefully did *not* make the position responsible to social services, and
specified that the administrator "co-ordinates with the State Department of
Social Services regarding alternatives to placement, including fiscal procedures
. . . reporting procedures . . . and outcome measures . . ." Tasks also included
the preparation of yearly plans and amendments, and the implementation of
administrative policies necessary to carry out the plan with the administrator
acting "at the direction of the PAC" (SYP, 139). Tension seemed high in the
meeting and after some discussion the director of social services announced,
"We do not approve the position of staff administrator. Let's move on." The
leader of the team volunteered to help the supervisor rewrite the description
for the next meeting (SYP, 137).

At the next meeting, discussion of the administrator position again took
place in an atmosphere charged with tension. The revised job description was
presented, and it recommended a higher level position, specifically a Level III

in the County Merit System; salary $1,557/month, who would report "directly to the Chairman of the Placement Alternative Commission and receive overall supervision from the PAC" (SYP, 167). But the two PAC members who were responsible never had a chance to discuss it. Before they could speak, the director of social services announced that *they* had solved the problem. Instead of seeking a higher level administrator, as the revised job description recommended, they would take the available salary and split it between a lower rank administrator I position and a clerk typist. The director of one of the mental health centers chimed in in agreement (SYP, 164). The team leader protested that the new job description should be discussed *before* matters of money were debated. He also pointed out that commission members had originally envisioned someone at a higher level (SYP, 164).

The director disagreed. "We can't do that," he said. "I can't commit any more social service staff time to PAC. We have spent too much time already and have other things to do."

"The quality of the adolescent supervisor's work for the Commission has been very high," argued the team leader and the supervisor for juvenile probation. "We need someone at his level as staff administrator."

"The PAC has to have a secretary and it can't have a secretary if we try to get an Administrator III," countered the director of social services.

Several PAC members objected.

"Does the Commission feel it needs help?" asked the director.

"Yes, yes," everyone agreed, "but we need competent help, someone with independence and initiative." The director intimated that if PAC wanted a staff person it would have to be on his terms or not at all and moved for adjournment (SYP, 165).

At the next meeting, the head of the detention center started off discussion about the PAC administrator by saying that he had been thinking since last week and had talked to several commission members and had concluded that the plan proposed last week by the director of social services was a good one. He moved that PAC adopt it. The mental health director who had supported the director of social services the previous week seconded the motion.

The chief probation officer began waving the job description from the previous meeting, "We should talk about this description before we decide," he said.

An involved discussion ensued about the relative salaries and job descriptions for Administrators I, II, and III. The social services adolescent supervisor was asked if he would consider the job; but he said he had just resigned from social services to take another job.

When the vote was called, there was some question about what the motion was, whether the group was ready to vote, and who was entitled to vote. The chief probation officer made it clear that he would vote against the motion. After much confusion, the social services director announced that the vote was 5 to 4 in favor of the motion. Everyone but the director of social services looked puzzled, as they tried to count hands and figure out just what had passed. The Commission moved on to other business (SYP, 205).

Two weeks later, one of the mental health directors and the chief probation officer announced to PAC that they had interviewed a very good candidate for the staff administrator position and recommended that PAC hire her. She was currently an administrative secretary from a social services department in another county. Since the candidate was already an Administrative Secretary, the director of social services suggested they change the job to that level, and he could have her transferred over to his department very quickly.

The candidate's present salary was more than that allocated for the PAC position, but PAC would not need to hire a secretary because the candidate was a secretary and could do her own typing (SYP, 246). With almost no discussion, the group voted affirmatively and PAC had their new administrator. She was housed within social services, reported to the director of social services, and became the senior administrative secretary for the department a few months later when that position became available (SYP, 757).

It was hard to understand at the time just why the decision about the PAC administrator became such an emotionally charged issue. The four people working consistently for a strong administrator were the two probation officers, the diagnostic team leader, and the social services staff member who left to take another job. The split was not simply along organizational lines, except for probation. It appeared almost to be a case of the child savers against the bureaucrats. It is likely that a young professional administrator who was a strong child advocate, especially in coalition with the team leader and the probation officers, would have posed a serious threat to the control of PAC maintained by the director of social services. The judge and social services often were in disagreement over placement decisions, and it was not yet clear just how the new legislation would affect the balance of power between them. If the director of social services was going to maximize his control over his budget, it was important for him to maintain control over the PAC. At least in the first two years, he was successful in doing so.

In the Child's Best Interest?

Again and again in PAC meetings, the legislation to reduce out-of-home placement was posed as being in opposition to the best interest of the child.

A probation officer called it "essentially a piece of negative legislation" (SYP, 504), and one PAC member asked, "Are we required to select the 'best' treatment for a kid, as we have in the past when we operated on the 'best interests of the child principle'? Or are we required to select the 'least restrictive' treatment" (SYP, 386).

Of course, least restrictive does not necessarily mean *best*, and although the legislation itself specified that placement should be "in the best interests of the child and the community," there was nevertheless some concern among PAC members that the law tipped the balance in favor of the least expensive treatment, even though this may not have been the legislation's intent. These worries surfaced almost weekly in PAC meetings.

PAC's First Year

In July after the new programs were launched and needed less attention, PAC decided to meet every other week instead of weekly. At the same time, some members tried to turn the commission's attention to a discussion of long-range goals. As one member put it, "We've been in operation almost a year. Perhaps it would be good to look back over our minutes and talk about what the Commission should be doing. We come to meetings and talk about a little bit of this and a little bit of that and somehow never really get the whole picture."

"We need to think about things that will be occurring over the next several years in the county," agreed the juvenile probation officer. "Much of what we have been doing is short range. If the Commission wants to have an impact it should think about long range planning" (SYP, 544–545).

The director of social services appointed the chief probation officer to chair a committee to look into long-range goals and such issues as group homes and special support for families whose children remain at home. The topic was never really picked up on by the group as a whole, however, and over time, PAC members seemed content to limit their jurisdiction to the county plan and its programs. As a result, the group's potential role as a serious policy making body never really materialized.

The original goals for the PAC, however, were fairly well met. The Commission submitted the plans, addenda to plans, and paperwork required by the state and made the decisions necessary to initiate and terminate programs for which it was responsible. As the next chapter will demonstrate, it also served as a forum for discussing practical problems experienced by the new programs.

Beyond this, however, the PACs goals and accomplishments are less easily enumerated. Members had different and sometimes conflicting ideas about what the commission could and should do. Social services clearly hoped to keep the commission under its control, and at the end of its first year it appeared to be safely within the social services domain. Probation and the head of the diagnostic team had pushed PAC to take the lead in expanding the variety of services available to youths, but they had met resistance, rising in part from limited energy. The network had experienced several years of change and people were tired. It was hard enough to do what had to be done, much less plan for more change.

The meetings allowed for discussion of issues raised by the new legislation, especially the question as to whether the principle of best interest of the child had been weakened by a requirement for least restrictive placement. But it was unclear just what impact these discussions had had on policies or actions of PAC participants.

In sum, PAC was too closely tied to social services and the status quo to raise an independent voice for children or move in innovative directions. Its members were too overextended to be able to put time and energy into creative thinking about new ways of doing things. Human resources, like financial resources, were already stretched too thin. The old dreams, like 'best interest of the child' were falling away, and there were not enough resources available to create new ones.

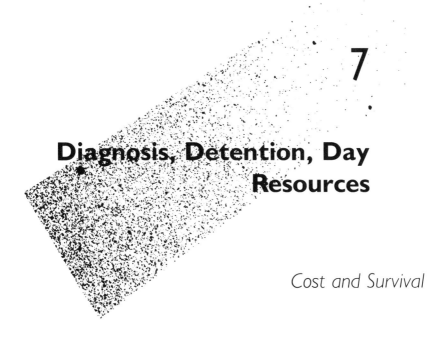

Diagnosis, Detention, Day Resources

Cost and Survival

Decisions about the treatment of troubled children are influenced by the nature of available facilities, which is influenced in turn by legislative and organizational factors and by the court network's capacity to develop and implement services. The new legislation to reduce out-of-home placement changed the rules in the state for the provision and financing of services for juveniles as well as the criteria for placement. Members of the Placement Alternatives Commission negotiated the meaning of these new rules for Suburban County as they worked with three programs—the detention alternatives program, the diagnostic team, and the day resource center—that provided the basis for its new system of services.

In spite of the great optimism with which all three were launched, only one was viewed positively in Suburban County a year later. Each had organizational, economic, and political vulnerabilities that made survival or success problematic. Their brief histories raise questions about the creation and implementation of change and about the impact of bureaucratic and resource issues on decision making.

Detention Alternatives Program

The detention alternatives program was designed to reduce pretrial detention of juveniles, especially in secure facilities. A federally funded demonstration project, it reflected a national concern about large numbers of children held in jails and other secure facilities while waiting for their cases to be decided. Specifically, the project's goal was to reduce the population in Suburban County's juvenile detention center, which had been overcrowded for some time. The program was developed by the state but was organizationally intertwined with the other Suburban County programs because its coordinator was the leader of the diagnostic team and its practices brought it into daily contact with police officers, probation officers, and other court workers.

Detention had been a major issue in Suburban County even before the 1974 report that suggested the county was needlessly detaining youths. The acquisition of its own juvenile detention facilities in 1962 and the purchase of a larger building in 1966 were important steps forward for the court. But the issue was further aggravated by long case processing times. Most detained youths were out of detention within a week, but a few were not, and the expanding court population, coupled with lengthening case processing times, posed a potentially explosive detention problem in the near future.

The detention alternatives effort included two main components: a set of written criteria for detaining children and an intake unit at the detention center in which youth service workers screened children for admission using the criteria, provided crisis intervention services, and tried to locate nonsecure housing whenever possible for youths who could not return home.

The coordinator's dual role, head of both the detention alternatives program and the diagnostic team, was a source of ongoing confusion to PAC members and agency workers. Although selected by the PAC and supposedly responsible to it because of his position as leader of the diagnostic team, the coordinator was on the state payroll and reported to the Director of the Youth Detention Center, his direct supervisor within the state system (SYP, 161). PAC members were generally more aware of his work for the diagnostic team than his work on the detention alternatives program. They assumed that since PAC was responsible for the Diagnostic Team, its leader was responsible to PAC. They did not begin to focus on the organizational implications and potentially conflicting aspects of the two leadership roles until months after the programs got under way. They then began to complain that state tasks on the detention alternatives project had depleted too much of the coordinator's time, leaving too little for the Diagnostic Team.

Development of Nonsecure Alternatives to Detention

Juveniles pose special detention problems. Adults who are not dangerous to themselves or others can be released after arrest, either on their own recognizance or bail, even if they do not have anywhere to go. Juveniles, on the other hand, are supposed to be handed over to responsible adults, preferably their parents. If parents are not available or refuse to come collect their offspring, the child may have to be detained, even when there are no other reasons for such action. If the only holding facilities available for juveniles are locked facilities, then all detained youths must be placed there, even if they do not warrant such extreme measures. Access to the nonsecure shelter was particularly important for the estimated 30 percent of children who were held in detention because their parents did not want them back or could not be found, or the child refused to return home. Many youths were "good risks" and could be placed in less restrictive settings if such settings were available (SYP, 120). Suburban County had one nonsecure shelter facility in addition to the detention center, but it was usually full, so unavailable for arrested youths.

One of the goals of the detention alternatives program was to expand pretrial placement options for children. In its first several months, it brought about the licensing of three foster homes, each with one bed, in what was called the "Family Shelter program" (SYP, 580). It also developed a home detention program that provided support services of up to 30 days for parents who otherwise would be unable to keep their children at home while they waited for their cases to come up in court (SYP, 287). It also worked to open the children's shelter to arrested youths. This attempt, as well as some other efforts to expand alternatives, disrupted operating procedures in some organizations.

One problem with these solutions was transportation. The coordinator of the detention alternatives program articulated what most employees in the county tacitly understood: keeping youths out of detention was sometimes a simple matter of transportation. The detention center was in the western part of the county, comparatively close to the court, while the main nonsecure shelter facility was in the eastern end of the county. Police officers from municipalities near the detention center sometimes preferred it because it was more convenient and took less transportation time.

Availability of shelter space was also related to agency turf and budgets. The state controlled and paid for the detention center; social services controlled and paid for shelters. As a result, social services had to approve all admissions to shelters and sometimes denied it to youths accused of delinquency, ostensibly because they were too disruptive.

Part of the conflict about use of shelter facilities for youths with delinquency charges revolved around the recurrent problem about whether delinquents were children or offenders. Accused offenders often needed places to stay for the same reasons that neglected children did—there was no one at home to come get them or take care of them. Children similar on a variety of factors—previous number of arrests, disruptiveness, age, school experiences, difficult home conditions—were differentially welcomed into the shelter depending on their status as offender or child rather than their need.

A third problem, others felt, was that this denial was a means of keeping down costs charged to the social services budget. (Also, shelter space was sometimes unavailable to county youths because the shelter made all its empty beds available, on a paying basis, to children from other counties.) As a solution to this problem, the detention alternatives program attempted regularly to reserve a shelter bed for county youths, but this scheme met with some resistance.

The coordinator of the detention program grappled with the organizational and ideological limitations on nonsecure detention alternatives, and worked as an advocate to create a greater variety of short term facilities around the county. Since most of the short term resources—shelters, group homes, short-term foster homes—lay within the purview and financial expenditure of the social services department, the potential for conflict between the state-initiated detention program and the county director of social services was high. In Suburban County, the problem was exacerbated because the coordinator, who was new to the state and had few ties to the local network, had a lot of autonomy in his organizational role. He also had a strong personality and was an innovator and a doer, and his efforts to substitute use of shelter for detention rocked some boats.

Population Pressures in the Detention Center

Suburban County had been selected for the detention alternatives program in part because of the severely overcrowded conditions in its juvenile detention center. The center's maximum capacity was 15, which had been adequate in its earlier days, but now youths had to be transferred on an almost daily basis to the larger center in a nearby city. Since the 1974 report on adolescent services

services in the county (SYP, 1123), state budget committees had even suggested closing the center on several occasions because it was the smallest and least efficient unit in the state.

Threats to close the center usually were countered by proposals to build a new one. In 1977, the Youth Services Council, formed as a result of the 1974 report, presented a plan to the state legislature's Joint Budget Committee for a new multi-use complex that included detention facilities (SYPN, 25–27). The plan had not materialized, but the need for a new larger center continued to be discussed even as county officials hoped that the detention alternative program would make a new building unnecessary.

In light of almost yearly efforts to close the detention center, it is surprising that PAC members and other agency workers focused on the need for a new center rather than on the possibility of the old center closing. In retrospect, it is hard to understand how they could have viewed the county's selection as the site for the detention alternatives program with so little sense of threat.

Institution of Formal Criteria for Detention

Shortly after the detention alternatives program went into operation, it moved to set up formal written criteria for detention. The director of the youth detention center surprised the PAC meeting in early March by announcing that he, the state DOI staff members to whom he reported, and the newly hired coordinator of the detention alternatives program had had a meeting with the judge, who had agreed to a 90-day trial of a detention plan that included fairly stringent criteria for admission to the detention center. Resistance was immediate, especially from the probation representatives (SYP, 205). PAC members were stunned that this had been proposed and agreed to without their involvement or knowledge. The juvenile probation supervisor argued, for example, that the judge should not have made such an agreement without the involvement of probation, whose workers had a "hands on" sense of whether the changes made sense.

"We would just like to know that this kind of thing won't happen again," the chief probation officer added after heated discussion (SYP 206). But that assurance was not forthcoming.

The tension over the detention criteria went on through several meetings. It was implied that probation was using detention inappropriately, as short-term punishment to bring unruly youths into line, which was vehemently denied by the representatives of both probation and the detention staff in PAC meetings (SYP, 245, 353). In addition, the dual organizational role played by the director of the detention alternatives program confused everyone. As a state employee responsible for the program, his visit to the judge was appropriate; as leader of the diagnostic team, however, it was not. There were also some organizational dimensions to probation's animosity. Since probation was a state agency, and part of the state judicial department, its exclusion from a meeting between the judge and representatives of another state executive agency could be construed as an organizational affront.

Probation workers told our researchers that initially they had had little negative feeling about the detention alternatives program. After it got under way, however, competition between probation officers and detention intake staff members began to mount as they took differing positions on the needs of individual children. The relationships between the two agencies became increasingly strained as probation officers came to feel that the detention intake workers wanted children *out* of detention at all costs, and the intake workers felt that probation workers wanted children *in* detention, whether it was appropriate or not. Relations between the juvenile probation supervisor and the coordinator of the detention program also cooled. Two competent leaders, similar in philosophy and both concerned about youths and change within the system, moved from potential alliance to noninvolvement and disaffiliation.

In spite of the heated discussions and memo wars, the detention reduction plan moved ahead, essentially as outlined in the March meeting with the judge. The procedures followed in the 90-day trial became standard, and the detention center's population began to drop almost at once—and remained down. It was no longer necessary to transfer local youths to other facilities because of overcrowding. A comparison of April and May population figures for 1979 and 1980 for Suburban County and a nearby county showed that Suburban County had substantially reduced its detention population (SYP, 284).

There were no sounds of alarm in PAC meetings about the possible repercussions of these reductions on the county. Even when the director of the center warned in May, "We're able to refer 60% of the kids out of the center. Pretty soon we'll have to close it because we won't have anyone there," no one picked up on his message (SYP, 388). About half of the youths screened out of detention were sent home, and about a third went to shelters or group homes (SYP, 706). Measured in terms of a reduced detention population, then, the detention alternatives program was a success.

The Closing of the Detention Center

From Suburban County's point of view, however, it was not a success. Almost exactly a year after the program first got under way, the state *closed* Suburban

County's detention center, sending county youths to a nearby city. The county   99
was back to where it had been in the early 1960s—sending its children elsewhere for detention. The locally based center had important symbolic meaning
to the community as well as practical value, and its closing represented a blow
to local autonomy and control.

From the state's point of view, however, the closing made sense. State
budget officials ordered the Division of Youth Services to cut its annual budget
by $280,000, coincidentally the exact amount it took to operate the center in
Suburban County. At capacity, the center cost $18,831 per youth per year to
operate. With the success of the alternatives program and the resulting lower
daily census, however the cost per youth had skyrocketed to $31,319 (SYPN,
199; SYP, 207). Officials claimed they did not want to close the center, but
the center, with its high cost and low population, was expendable. County
officials, on the other hand, estimated that closing the center would mean an
additional $150,000 a year in transportation costs, to be assumed by the county.
The state saved money, but the county would have to pay the difference
(SYPN, 200).

Apart from financial concerns, county citizens and officials also worried
about the effect of detention in the city on local youths. They were concerned
that the children lacked the survival skills necessary to cope with a large facility
and adolescents believed to be largely streetwise "minority toughs" (SYPN,
1). They also feared that the local youths would become isolated since it would
be harder for attorneys, probation officers, and family members to visit them.
Consequently, there was a brief flurry of activity to rally support to keep the
center open, including some public meetings, a letter writing campaign, and
news coverage. The District Attorney met with Republican legislators in the
county to try to generate support, but to no avail. The efforts to stave off
closure of the detention center failed. The county felt that it had been punished
for conducting a successful program, and its relationships with the state, which
was tenuous at best, deteriorated further.

Youth Diagnostic Team

The Diagnostic Team's task was to evaluate every child recommended for
out-of-home placement. Its goals were to reduce the number of youths placed
out-of-home; reduce overall length of stay in placement; and utilize the least
restrictive program available, hopefully within the community (SYP, 759).
The evaluation itself consisted of several parts: a family/social evaluation in
which referring professionals and team members discussed the need for place-

ment and possible treatment plans with the family and child; a medical examination; educational review of prior school performance, ability, and achievement; and psychological interviews and testing. A treatment team, including the referring professionals, developed a recommendation for the youth and family and a report was written for the judge who then reviewed the case and made the final decision.

The Youth Diagnostic Team, or "Team", was a source of dissatisfaction and confusion from its inception and took an inordinate amount of PAC time. Although proposed in the county plan as a part of the program to reduce out-of-home placement, it was also part of the same federally funded package as the detention alternatives program and was administered by the coordinator of that program. The staff of the diagnostic team included the team leader and secretary, funded through the federal grant, a caseworker from social services, psychologists from the two mental health centers, a nurse from the community health center, and an educational diagnostician.

In addition to doing full-scale evaluations, the diagnostic team reviewed and visited existing residential programs for youths. They also did six-month placement reviews, as well as other less elaborate evaluations of youths brought into custody, including one hour assessments on children whose parents called seeking help (SYP, 285–286). These short evaluations were a source of conflict from the beginning and the team worked hard to divest itself of them. Initially they were able to handle only four full evaluations a week. When backlogs began to develop, PAC urged them to take on six. In return, the leader asked if the team could be relieved of the short, "voluntary" evaluations, and arrangements were made to hire two youth service workers to do them at the detention center. This freed the diagnostic team to concentrate on the full-scale placement evaluations. Among PAC members, a sense developed early that the diagnostic team was not doing enough work. Team members, on the other hand, felt that they were being pushed too hard.

The debate over the team's workload and procedures was partly a legacy it acquired from an earlier interdisciplinary team that had been responsible for the evaluation of status offenders before they were eliminated in July 1979. Because of its similarity to its predecessor, the new team inherited the dissatisfactions and expectations some county workers had regarding the old (SYP, 162). The directors of the two mental health centers in particular had been unhappy about what they perceived as the earlier team's low workload and expressed similar concerns about the diagnostic team.

Probation, which had had substantial imput into the earlier team, had been left out of the new one altogether. Probation officers kept harking back to the positive aspects of the earlier team and seemed to expect the new one to be similar and to provide them with the same access to team evaluations that they had previously enjoyed.

Organizational Limitations of the Team

The diagnostic team was an organizational nightmare, encompassing members of autonomous agencies who competed with each other for resources and clients. It was viewed by agencies as an organizational Siberia, a place to assign troublesome workers. Some salaries came from federal grant money, others came from state start-up funds or local agency budgets. Workers had different pay scales and even different holidays. The way the team had been set up, none of the members were organizationally responsible to the leader, even though he was responsible for the outcome of their work.

The diagnostic team's organizational position, and its lack of independent existence apart from the agencies who provided it with staff, created other serious problems. It had no budget of its own and was dependent on its host agencies (social services especially) for everything, even supplies. Equipment needed by the nurse to do physical examinations became a political problem early in the team's development, for example. Several heated disputes erupted in PAC, and one meeting was precipitously adjourned after sharp words passed between the director of social services and a doctor from the medical center over who would provide the medical equipment. (The issue was eventually resolved by an offer of discarded equipment from one of the mental health centers.) After 5 months, the team leader was still trying to get a locked filing cabinet, and complained that the present system kept him constantly indebted to social services. "It's just one more way to keep control over me," he concluded (SYP, 246).

Indeed, the diagnostic team posed a special threat to social services because it held potential control over placements for which social services had to pay. The team leader, outspoken and assertive, made it clear that he was not a social services partisan and quickly made it his business to develop a good relationship with the judge and talk individually with others in the juvenile justice network. His position as a state employee gave him an independent base, separate from either social services or the county juvenile court. His aggressive style was different from that of the director of social services, an experienced older man who was concerned about not making waves, holding the budget down, and keeping the county commissioners happy. Relations between the two men cooled soon after the leader was hired.

Others were also unhappy with the team. Probation officers felt that they now had less chance to have their clients evaluated for placement, since under the new scheme they were excluded from anything more than making a referral to social services. They also felt that the detention program took away much of their discretion in handling their probationers (SYP, 271), and since the same person coordinated both the detention program and the team, there may have been some spillover of bad feelings.

Mental health center directors seemed generally unhappy with the team as well, although their reasons were not as clear. Perhaps the mental health directors were concerned about where the money for the team would come from when the federal grant ran out at the end of the year, and saw it as an eventual competitor with the day resource centers, to which they were deeply committed.

Team's Role as Protector of the Child's Best Interest

By May, PAC members, especially the mental health center directors, were expressing concern that the team did not have the right philosophy about placement. The team, some PAC members worried, was still operating on the "best interest of the child" principle rather than the principle of "least restrictive placement." Social services and the PAC saw the team as an instrument for reducing out-of-home placement, and providing the flow of cases to the new day resource centers. The director of social services made this point clearly even before the first day resource center opened. "If the team isn't committed to the day treatment center," he remarked, "we can't afford it" (SYP, 386).

Line workers in probation and social services saw the team as the route toward getting needed intensive treatment for children and, not incidentally, as a means of moving difficult children out of their own overwhelming caseloads (SYP, 271, 387). Finally, the team saw itself as a group of professionals providing a full-scale evaluation to diagnose needs and prescribe treatment in the child's best interest. They were finding, as other agencies have discovered, that the more thorough the evaluation, the more needs the evaluation group can identify. The more needs there are, the better case a professional can make for placement as opposed to nonplacement.

The dissatisfaction surrounding the team was due in part to the discomfort caused by the new legislation to reduce out-of-home placement. The team, in fact, may have become the scapegoat for unhappiness and confusion about the legislation. As the year wore on, the need for support services and more

good foster homes and nonsecure residential facilities in the community became
evident (SYP, 387), but the only new program in the county was the day
resource center with places for 15 youths. What good did it do to have a
diagnostic team capable of designing a highly individualized treatment program when there were so few treatment options?

The "political football" case mentioned earlier, involving the team's only
out-of-state placement recommendation, illustrated the way in which the team's
decisions were undermined by lack of resources and external constraints. In
that case, all the county agencies stood solidly together behind the local decision, but the messages from the state were not lost on county professionals.
Cost was important, more important perhaps than what evaluation teams and
judges thought about an individual child's best interest. And the state was
monitoring cost in a way it had not monitored it before.

Conflict Between the Team and PAC

In early June, the PAC's dissatisfaction with the team reached its peak. First,
agencies with a member on the team were asked to talk to the member they
"owned" and interpret to them the PAC's philosophy about placement. Then
at the suggestion of one of the mental health center directors, a joint meeting
between PAC and the team was scheduled in late June (SYP, 387). The purpose
of the meeting was to make it clear to the team what was expected of it. When
asked the day before the meeting what he thought would happen, the team
leader told a researcher that it would either be a negative meeting or everyone
would sit around and ask why they were getting together (SYP, 454). It turned
out to be more the latter than the former.

Team members went into the meeting prepared to talk about what they
did for the team and their ideas about what kinds of placement facilities were
necessary. They were puzzled that they were not given an opportunity to do
this or express their opinions, and said afterwards that they did not understand
why the meeting had been called and why they were there (SYP, 451–455).
They were not alone in their confusion. The meeting did not appear to have
a clear focus and covered a wide range of topics rather unsystematically. At
one point the chief probation officer said, "I've been away from a few meetings,
can someone please inform me of the purpose of this meeting" (SYP, 454).

Team members said afterward that the PAC members made statements
that obviously showed that they had not read the team reports that had been
given to them in advance and were unaware of what the team actually did.
They were discouraged after the meeting and most felt that the team would

not last much longer, in part because it would not be able to reduce costs enough. Individuals began to plan what they would do next, after the team was disbanded (SYP, 455).

The Team's Demise

Conflict between the team and social services over placements continued. Shortly after the June meeting, the team recommended placement for a juvenile in a structured residential facility, but the placement was not approved by social services and the case was sent back to the team for review. The team stuck to its recommendation in a heated and tense meeting, but social services went ahead and used a less restrictive setting, from which the child ran away after four days (SYP, 519). In August, Social Services reduced the time of its caseworker on the team from five days a week to four (SYP, 561).

Around the same time, one of the mental health directors suggested in a PAC meeting that, in order to fill the new day resource center, social services should temporarily refer youths directly to the center without having them evaluated. The director of the center, which had seven youths at the time, objected. She felt the team's evaluations were useful and she was not equipped to do such work on her own. Some PAC members were also uncomfortable with the proposal, (SYP, 561), but the direct referral system was approved and remained in effect for almost two months, until the center was full.

As the team moved toward the end of its year of federal funding, state officials made it clear that it would soon be without a leader or funds unless county officials took action. The leader was scheduled to leave January 1 to assume other duties for the state outside Suburban County. Federal funds for the rest of the team expired in March. Even before the end of the year, the team leader spent time traveling to other parts of the state to publicize the now highly touted detention alternatives program and to lay the groundwork for similar programs in other counties. There was some discussion about the state providing continuing funding, but the state made it clear that $12,000 was the maximum it could commit (SYP, 694–695).

After considerable discussion, the PAC temporarily put the director of the day resource center in charge of the team, despite her objections that she already had more than a full-time job (SYP, 756). The PAC further agreed that when the director of the second day resource center started work in early February, she would temporarily supervise the team until the PAC could decide what to do about it. In the meantime, the commission asked one of the mental health directors to review all the cases referred to the team and report results and recommendations.

For the next few months the team limped along, demoralized and essentially leaderless. Members felt they were being asked too often by social services to reevaluate their initial recommendations because their recommended placements were too expensive. Social services vehemently denied this and the PAC went on record as agreeing that this was not true. The judge, on the other hand, continued to rely on the team, accept its recommendations, and see it essentially as "his" team—although he was not in a position to fund it (SYP, 790–791).

In March 1981, the mental health center director reported on the team and its clients, and the results give a sense of the multifaceted problems children encounter before the court. Most of the 173 youths referred for evaluation were not new to human services. Almost half had already been adjudicated delinquent before referral. Another half had had prior placements out of the home. Forty percent had been seen at one of the mental health centers and 20 percent had a history of psychiatric hospitalization. A third had had a full psychological test work-up and evaluation within 18 months of referral (SYP, 823–824).

On the basis of this information, the director of the mental health center argued that a great deal already was known about many youths who were evaluated by the team. He recommended to PAC that the evaluations be decentralized back to the original agencies and that the team should function as a coordinating mechanism rather than a diagnostic service. Along these lines, he recommended that a coordinator be hired by social services to take referrals, coordinate the staffing meetings, and appear in court with evaluations and recommendations. Although the new structure would not provide as complete and thorough evaluations as before, he argued that it would provide an adequate evaluation to accomplish the purposes required by the new legislation (SYP, 424A).

The recommendation was adopted. In May, the team secretary and equipment moved to social services. The team as an independent entity ceased to exist, although, as PAC members were quick to note, it had not been disbanded, just decentralized (SYP, 887). In mid-August 1981, a year after recommendations had been made to bypass the team in making decisions about candidates for the day treatment center, the team did cease to exist altogether, and its functions were merged into a foster care team that operated within social services. A new team, the crisis shelter team, was formed to provide services to youths in crisis.

The diagnostic team originally had been seen as a means of reducing placement costs, but it proved to be less useful in this regard than had been anticipated. The new legislation mandated some kind of interdisciplinary evaluation of youths who were being considered for placement. The placement study carried out prior to the drafting of the legislation actually included a detailed description of a proposed diagnostic team that was almost identical to the one set up in Suburban County. On paper it looked good, but in practice the team's organizational structure was fraught with problems. In addition, although it was able to screen youths to identify those most appropriate for the day resource center, its work in this area was undermined by the decision to bypass it at a time when the center needed to reach capacity quickly. Overall, it identified more needs of county children than the county wanted to acknowledge.

It is clear from the summary of the charts done at the end of February that the majority of youths referred to the team had many problems and a substantial history of prior involvement with service agencies. Most were good candidates for out-of-home placement on several dimensions. Thus, it is not surprising that the team was unpopular from the beginning. It continued to identify serious and deep needs of children at a time when it was politically unpopular to do so. PAC members complained that the team leader had never had the right approach at all, or, as one PAC member put it, "He was the Judge's man from the beginning. His goal was 'best interest.' We all knew what was going on, but we didn't do anything. We should have talked about all this a year ago" (SYP, 836).

In retrospect, it is hard to imagine just what Suburban County wanted from the diagnostic team or why anyone expected it to reduce placement costs sharply. Its very nature and composition, together with the nature of its referrals and the limitations of local treatment options, made it virtually impossible for the team to meet these expectations.

The Day Resource Centers

Of the three programs, only the day resource center could be seen as successful from the county's point of view. The county's plan called for two treatment centers, one in the east and one in the west. The director of social services and PAC decided to commit funds to only one at first. If it was successful, they would develop the second one.

The day centers were based on the premise that many youths are placed in residential facilities simply because there are no intensive adolescent programs available that provide family support and treatment for youths living at home. Youths were expected to enter the center after being evaluated by the youth diagnostic team. Prerequisites for acceptance included a family capable of participation in treatment: a history of social, interactional, or peer difficulties: a history of school problems: and the absence of severe psychosis. For each child, an individual treatment plan was set up.

The day treatment program encompassed an 8½ hour day with clients present for approximately 6½ hours. The morning was spent in basic academics. After lunch, the emphasis was on vocational training, supervised placements, and daily group therapy. At least once a week each family was seen together in treatment. The program included a transportation system so that youths' attendance was not dependent on their own initiative or their parents' degree of investment in the treatment (SYP, 30).

The program was aimed at serving adolescents who could not attend even special school programs or maintain themselves at home. The objectives included lowering the level of out-of-home placements by a monthly average of 30 youths who would be served by the two day treatment programs, and reducing the county's average length of stay in out-of-home placement by 5 percent below the previous fiscal year.

Once it was clear that the plan had been approved and state start-up money would be available to social services for a day resource center, PAC discussions centered on its organizational framework. What kind of person would run the center and who would that person be responsible to? Several organizational alternatives were considered. The state discouraged the inclusion of day resource centers within social services, even though the money and referrals went through them, and PAC members generally agreed that they should be housed elsewhere. There was talk of having the mental health centers take on the programs, but some PAC members worried that close association with a mental health facility would somehow taint the centers and stigmatize the children. At one meeting in early February, the director of social services suggested contracting the running of the centers to an outside organization.

Suddenly by the February 20th PAC meeting, all the basic organizational issues had been resolved (SYP, 134). PAC agreed that the day resource programs would be run through the mental health centers with a contract from social services. Representatives from social services and the mental health centers had already located two possible spaces to house the first program— one in the same building as the East Side mental health center and the other across the street. PAC members decided on the space within the mental health center building and agreed to hold their next meeting there to look at it. A position announcement for the coordinator of the center was circulated for discussion and approved.

What brought this swift resolution? One reason was the simple need to get the program going. Pressure was already building to get placements and costs down. But there were other less visible reasons. State officials who viewed the new legislation as a means toward the development of innovative options for treatment were trying to use it to get community mental health centers more involved with adolescents. Toward this end, a group of directors from three community mental health centers and a state official from the Department of Institutions began work early in the year to develop plans to motivate mental health centers and departments of social services throughout the state to develop joint programs for youths at risk of out-of-home placement. Two of these directors were associated with the centers in Suburban County (SYP, 1158). The motivators were substantial. They involved the use of federal medicaid dollars for youths in jointly developed nonresidential programs. If the plan succeeded, both social services and the mental health centers stood to gain substantially increased resources for services.

When a decision about the first day resource center was made, these arrangements were still in process. If the medicaid dollars came through, both social services and the mental health centers would substantially augment their resources. Neither could gain the resources without the other. The directors of Suburban County's mental health centers had a high stake in maintaining good relationships with social services because its director controlled the start-up money for the new programs and, with PAC, made the decision about what agency would run them.

Pressures to Reach Capacity

Even before the first center opened, there was concern about whether the team was referring enough children to it and whether it would fill up quickly enough. In June, social services, at the request of PAC, drew up a list of adolescents already in placement who might be suitable for transfer into the center. The director of the day resource center opposed the plan, arguing that re-placed youths were harder to treat than those who were newly placed. Nevertheless, PAC made arrangements to move ahead at once with replacement. At the June 4th meeting, one member suggested that social services provide a list of possible candidates for re-placement to the diagnostic team by June 11, have the team review them and make decisions within a week, and move them into the center by July 1. Again, the director of the day resource center demurred. She felt the deadline would not allow enough time for the youths' present counselors to prepare them for the change (SYP, 416).

In spite of the director's concerns, the idea of a quickly accomplished placement combination of "front end" (new) youths and "back end" (already placed) youths gained momentum over the week. Commission members met with the judge who was receptive to the plan but not to the suggested timeframe. His dissatisfaction with the proposed schedule centered on the impact on his already-heavy court caseload of the extra reviews necessary to move the children from residential to home placement. The supervisor of the adolescent program in social services reviewed cases in placement and found five appropriate for referral to the day resource center. She also found several she felt could be sent directly home (SYP, 424).

Even with these concentrated efforts of PAC the center acquired clients slowly. A month after it opened, it had only three youths participating, with three more scheduled to start. Fifteen youths had been referred, but nine had either not entered or not remained, usually because the youth was too disruptive or the parents uncooperative. One girl had been placed privately by her mother and another had run away (SYP, 503). A month later, the center was working with eight youths, including three re-placements.

In an effort to understand why utilization of the center remained so low, a committee of PAC members reviewed referrals with the center's director. The review identified only two additional youths that the director felt she might have accepted on a trial basis, the rest were either too disruptive, had parents who refused to be involved, or had gone somewhere else before she had ever seen them. Social services was concerned that the county was not saving placement money. At capacity, the cost of the center for each child would be $755 a month, but for only eight children, it was $1,174 per month, not substantially less than some residential placements (SYP, 543).

The issue about who should be referred to the center and the importance of its being at capacity came up again in a few weeks. PAC members asked the director if she felt pressure to keep kids longer than necessary in order to fill up the center. She said no, but she did feel pressure to keep kids who might do better in a residential child care facility. She felt, moreover, that lack of involvement by a child's family was usually a good predictor of how the child would respond; if a child *wanted* to be placed, he or she usually did not do well in the day program (SYP, 593, 636).

Unanticipated Problems of Community Programs

As the crisis of low enrollment subsided, at least temporarily, the center continued to operate in a highly volatile environment with ongoing resource limitations and unanticipated needs and problems. Soon after the center went into operation in June, for example, the director needed to get a child out of his home for a few days during a family crisis but had nowhere to house him.

The children's shelter, as usual, was full, with a waiting period of five days (SYP, 494). She brought the problem to PAC, and eventually financial and residential arrangements were worked out for emergencies.

In spite of the center's focus on family support services, only its director had experience in family counseling. The other staff members, whose annual salaries were budgeted at between $10,000 and $12,000, had little or no training in counseling. The lack of resources put a heavy burden on the director of the center as she attempted to get the program started, carry all the family counseling, and train staff members. An able and dedicated woman, the director described her work in the center to a researcher as the most draining job she had ever had (SYP, 636). Clearly, an intensive community program had special staff needs and required substantial resources. These resources were not provided during this crucial start-up period and one wonders if anyone expected the center to succeed.

As the program matured and participants became ready to move back into regular schools, a new problem emerged. Many youths did not want to leave. The director asked PAC if there was any money to provide transitional services so that the adolescents returning to their schools could maintain some contact with the center for several weeks and continue in family and individual therapy during their adjustment periods. PAC members agreed that the request made sense, but under the old financial system there were no clear financial mechanisms for paying for services for youths once they left a program. They were either in a program, or out of it, and there did not seem to be any ground in between. Eventually this problem, too, was resolved as funding agencies made it possible for the center to bill for specific services as well as on a daily basis.

Who Pays for the Center's Educational Services?

Soon another threat to the center flared up—the dispute over who should pay its educational costs. The director of social services said he would close the center if educational authorities did not pay for a teacher. The authorities refused, and the center became a pawn in a battle that went far beyond its program or survival. The county requested initial start-up funds to cover costs of the special education teachers in each center and the team's educational diagnostician for the first several months. The school districts were not eager to pick up the cost of any of the educational components of either the centers or the team.

Schools, like social services and courts, were facing serious resource problems as well as adjustments to new and somewhat ambiguous legislation

(Public Law 94–142, the Handicapped Children's Education Act, for instance).   111
The law committed federal funds for only a small fraction of the educational expenses, it mandated, requiring states and local governments to sup-
ply the remainder (Jacobs, 1985). Schools found themselves responsible for
expensive programs in special education for many categories of children, including emotionally disturbed and learning disabled, two categories in which
delinquent children could easily fall. Jacobs (1985:13), in an analysis of the
impact of Public Law 94–142, pointed out that one effect of the legislation
was to displace from the federal government to the states conflict over the
special education costs of children placed for noneducational reasons. The
controversy that raged in Suburban County supported his point.

The legislation to reduce out-of-home placement posed additional problems for school districts. It was explicit that the educational costs of placement
were not placement costs, but must be borne by the educational institution in
the community in which the child lived. School districts, already beleaguered
by expanding populations, rising costs, and tax-weary citizens, feared that
they would become financially responsible not only for the costs of new
placement-based educational programs, developed under the new law, but also
for the educational programs in community-based programs. They also worried that they would be responsible for meeting special educational needs that
might be identified by agencies over which they had no control.

A cooperative educational services agency, which represented most of
the school districts in Suburban County, had a representative on PAC. Two
educational specialists who worked for the agency also appeared periodically
at PAC meetings. Their attitude toward the PAC was one of barely suppressed
hostility, since they seemed to perceive their role as an advocate for the schools
as an essentially adversarial position. Their participation in the meetings usually
involved a complex discussion of money, and often became a dialogue with
the director of social services about who would pay for the educational components of the programs, specifically the educational supplies, special education
teacher, teacher-aides in the day resource centers, and the educational diagnostician on the Team. The staff of the Day Resource Center ultimately paid
the price.

The school districts were particularly threatened by the educational and
psychological testing on the diagnostic team. In order to protect themselves
from having to provide services for youths who might be identified by the
Team as having special educational needs, local school districts made it clear
that they were liable only for conditions that the *school's* diagnosticians identified. One school district signalled its position shortly after the diagnostic
team started work with a sharp letter to PAC complaining that the diagnostic

team had been set up without consultation with the schools and that the educational diagnostician on the team duplicated services already provided by school districts within the county (SYP, 386).

As September 1980 approached, and start-up funds ran out, the directors of special education of the county denied the social services request for $82,000 to support the educational components in the day resource treatment centers and the educational diagnostician on the team. They did agree, however, to commit a maximum of $22,000 for educational services. PAC responded by sending an amendment of its 1981 county plan to the state Department of Social Services. It requested an increased allocation of $61,204 for funds for the educational portion of the two programs, with the $22,000 committed by the school districts representing the county's share of costs.

The budget battle began in earnest. The county director of social services admitted that he expected the request to be turned down, but that this would provide him with leverage against the state Department of Education. In early November, the request was indeed turned down, on the grounds that the funding of educational costs out of foster care money was inappropriate. A meeting of state and local officials was set to discuss the problem.

Day Resource Center—A Pawn in a Budget Battle

Meanwhile, the day resource center, still struggling through its first few months of existence, became a pawn in the budget battle. One teacher, worried that she would be without a job when funds ran out in December, began to look for a new position. The director of social services made it clear at a PAC meeting that he was prepared to disband both the center and the diagnostic team if educational agencies did not pay their share of the two programs (SYP, 695). This struck mainly at the center since the Team by this time had already been substantially undermined. Stunned PAC members and the Director of the Day Resource Center questioned the director of social services. What did he mean, he would disband the center? Questioning brought no reassurance. The director would not know anything, he said, until after the upcoming meeting (SYP, 695).

The educational representative made it clear that the school districts would not allow other agencies to commit educational funds. The PAC became a forum in which social services and the school districts established bargaining positions in preparation for the upcoming state-local meetings. The goal of local officials on both sides was to get the *state* department of education to provide funds for the educational components of the new programs.

Meanwhile, at the day resource center, uncertainty about the future cre-

ated growing morale problems for both adolescents and staff members (SYP,
694). They faced external threats of loss of funds and possible loss of a teacher,
the anxiety of several youths about to leave the center uncertain if any transition
services would be available, and Christmas, with all the tensions that major
holidays usually create for youths and adults.

The first meeting of social services and education led only to an agreement
to meet again in three weeks. One problem had become obvious: The special
education departments of local school districts had no idea what the day resource center and the team were doing or why education should be involved.
Once informed, they became more supportive of the day resource center,
while remaining generally unsupportive of the diagnostic team.

Suburban County was not alone in its conflict over the financing of educational services for new programs. Other counties were beginning to have
similar problems and were waiting to see how the issue was going to be
resolved in Suburban County. The educational representative observed with
a certain amount of glee that the state was just beginning to realize that this
was a "big bucks problem." In part, the problem was complicated by unclear
legislation. The new law to reduce out-of-home placement gave the responsibility for payment for community programs to social services, while the
Handicapped Act gave the responsibility for payment for education programs
to education.

The next round of meetings appeared to provide at least a temporary
victory to the county department of social services. The director reported
jubilantly to PAC at its December 17th meeting that it looked almost certain
that the county social services would not be paying for educational components
of the diagnostic team or the day resource centers. Ultimately they did not.
Educational costs in the day resource centers were paid for with educational
funds, just as they were in juvenile residential facilities.

Institutionalization of the Day Resource Centers

The center did not close, the teacher did not leave, Christmas passed, and the
problem of transitional services was resolved. In fact, the center was seen as
so successful that the second one was authorized and a search for its director
was started. The decision to go ahead with the second center was in a sense
the *rite de passage* of the day resource concept, and appeared to move both
centers into a more stable existence. The second director worked closely with
the first center and its director as she began to put together her staff and
program, providing needed support and relief.

By June 1981, the first center was attempting to take more difficult cases for a 60-day trial to see what its treatment limits were. It was given permission by PAC to take the same holidays as regular schools with a month off in the summer, rather than trying to function all year (SYP, 907). The second center took longer to move into operation than had been anticipated because renovation of its planned site moved more slowly and cost more than had been expected. It finally opened in temporary quarters, where it remained for over six months before moving into permanent spaces (SYP, 983).

Yet stability in the day resource centers could not be taken for granted. Program population again became an issue for the first center just a year after it opened, as the census dropped from nine in July to five in August and September. A major problem was that most of the adolescents who were being referred to the center had already had a full range of attempts at least-restrictive treatment that had proved unsuccessful. Population problems eased within a few months, when both centers were nearly full, but both continued to have a chronic problem with runaways (SYP, 1057). After a year and a half of operation, 41 youths had entered the two programs. Fifteen of these left the program to enter residential treatment programs and were classified as failures. Almost all of these youths had a strong history of neglect. They also were more likely to have temper problems and tendencies toward self-destruction (SYP, 1057). Day treatment of adolescents was not turning out to be easy.

Some Policy Issues

The story of the development of the day resource centers is instructive on several counts. The pressure on the centers to fill quickly and stay near capacity shows how the dynamics of treatment programs are driven by considerations of costs and political exigencies, no matter how concerned and dedicated referring professionals and staff members may be. The centers' difficulties in maintaining population and retaining youths who entered the program threw into question the premise that many youths placed in residential facilities can be maintained less expensively at home.

There may be a core group of children in any jurisdiction who need highly structured placement or to get away from home. Once a community decides to address the needs of that core group, it may not be able to reduce its residential population much further unless it makes *substantial* commitments to community programs that are almost equal to the cost of residential programs. For some children, there may be no cheap alternatives.

Least restrictive may *not* be synonymous with less expensive. Our assumption that the two go together, and our efforts to sell deinstitutionalization programs as cheaper, may have seriously limited our ability to fully develop the potential of nonresidential treatment programs. Our need to show reduced costs quickly and in absolute terms may doom these potentially innovative and successful programs to ultimate mediocrity, at best.

Another problem for the day resource centers may also have been that they did not have an established place in the political hierarchy of service agencies. Although under the umbrella of the mental health centers, they depended heavily upon social services for referrals and financing, and reported to the Placement Alternatives Commission. Thus, the directors did not have an independent power base from which to fend off external decisions with which they did not agree. As a result, the director's disagreement with the plan to refer youths to the center without having a diagnostic team evaluation went unheeded, as did her objection to the inclusion of children coming from residential placements, and to her appointment as leader of the diagnostic team.

In the day resource centers, as in so many parts of the juvenile justice system, responsibility for implementation of treatment was separate from fiscal responsibility and policy decision making. Here, as elsewhere, there was a strong tension between the need for enough discretion to allow individualization of treatment and the need for limitation of discretion in order to minimize abuse of power. Nevertheless, the PAC played a useful role in developing the day resource centers by providing a forum in which staff members of other agencies could be made aware of issues such as problems created by Medicare reimbursement and the need for crisis and transitional services for participants. In addition, the regular reports of the centers to PAC gave all the members a sense of involvement and vested interest in the success of the centers.

Impact of the Three Programs on the Court Network

The day resource centers, along with the detention alternatives program and the diagnostic team, all represented change brought into the juvenile justice system from the state and federal levels, primarily from new legislation. Over the course of the history of the three programs during the first year and a half after the legislation went into effect, participants in the court network moved through a variety of organizational alliances, the reasons for which were not always clear to an outsider.

There was a hesitation on the part of all participants to see social services get more budgetary and placement power than it already had. It appeared that the new legislation had actually increased the power of social services although this may not have been intended. In an environment of scarcity, the concept of "least restrictive" upon which the legislation had put its stamp of approval, could be read as "least expensive." Certainly, it placed more decisions about setting priorities in the hands of the agency that controlled the budget, in this case, social services. Even though the PAC members were unwilling to assign formal leadership of the Commission to the director of social services, it was obvious that his influence on the group was very strong, and that he understood and utilized his power. As one PAC member observed, "The director of social services has as much direct budget decisions as anyone in the system. He seems to have more power than anyone in PAC, probably because he has direct control over a very large budget" (SYP, 996).

The two directors of the mental health centers played maverick roles in PAC. On key issues they tended to align themselves with social services, but they had a secure independent base apart from the court and welfare system and were less involved in the ongoing operations of the court than some other participants. They took a strong negative stand against the diagnostic team almost from the beginning, but were always highly supportive of the day resource centers, which added to their organizational domain with minimum cost. It is interesting to note, however, that in these early months they referred no youths to the centers.

The real loser of organizational power as a result of the new legislation seemed to have been probation. The diagnostic team replaced a previous team designed to help status offenders that had been dominated by probation. As a result of the new procedures for recommending juveniles to the team for evaluation, probation officers felt that they had less access to placement than they had had before.

Probation officers also were affected by the detention alternatives program. The criteria for detention were taken to the judge and approved by him without their involvement. Individual probation officers felt that their discretion in the use of detention was being sharply limited and that their professional integrity was being subtly impugned. They were also one of the main losers when the local detention center closed because it became much more difficult for them to visit their clients.

Probation officers aligned themselves closely with the judge and saw themselves as an arm of the court. Although, like the judge, they were financially independent of local funds for salaries and organizational resources, they were highly dependent on local resources, especially social services, for placement of juveniles. They, along with the judge, saw themselves as protecting the best interests of the child, and in PAC conflicts always were in favor of more and better services for juveniles.

A year or so after the new legislation went into effect, the probation department underwent substantial reorganization and abandoned its specialized juvenile probation unit. It is interesting to speculate whether one underlying reason for this change might have been a decrease in the salience and satisfaction of the juvenile probation officers' roles, as a result of power realignments created by the new legislation.

8

Investment in the Future

From this study, it is clear that Suburban Court, like many juvenile courts in America, is dependent on its environment for legitimation, resources, and clientele. Although in the past we tended to think of the court as operating in isolation, this study documents the extent of the juvenile court's involvement in a network of legal and social services. Like other agencies, it competes for resources and clients and is affected by changing conditions on local and national levels. As we chart a course for the future of juvenile justice, we must take into account this context and address the interplay of funding decisions at federal, state, and local levels. By focusing primarily on the interaction between subunits of the court system—an interagency policy-making group, social services, probation, schools, experimental programs, mental health agencies, and state agencies responsible for substantial blocks of funding—this study attempted to show how their negotiations responded to and created changes and how these changes created the need for further negotiation and change.

The problems facing Suburban Court have no easy solutions. Years after our study, informal conversations with court workers suggest that not much has changed. There has been a high turnover in personnel (common in juvenile courts), an expansion of the day resource centers, some efforts to create new treatment programs, a chronic lack of funds, and unending worry about long case processing times. Conscientious, competent individuals continue to try to make a positive difference in the lives of troubled children and to protect the community from victimization. But the ideological, organizational, and economic context in which they work continues to make these goals difficult to attain.

What can we do? Community ambivalence, since the court's beginning in 1899, remains a key problem. What rights should children have? Who should be responsible for implementing them? There is no clear agreement. Although the court has become much more legalistic, the community remains undecided about whether it is a children's service agency or a court of law. It continues to send the court its problem children and expect magical solutions. The lack of clear priorities has allowed agencies in the court network great latitude in negotiating the nature of their objectives and operations, in spite of the apparent precision of legal language. In order to build an effective juvenile justice system we must first reduce community ambivalence and develop realistic expectations about what can be done for children who break the law.

We can help the court develop a more coherent set of goals in three ways. One is to acknowledge that delinquents are both children and offenders with accompanying recognition of the interests for community protection. A second means is to develop a comprehensive services policy for children that gives high priority to the needs of children before birth through adolescence. A third is to clarify the parameters of the juvenile court's responsibility to young offenders by establishing a graduated response system that depends on the seriousness and frequency of their offenses.

The Delinquent as Child and Offender

Ambivalence about whether juvenile offenders are to be considered as primarily children or offenders has plagued us since the juvenile court's inception. Early court reformers sought to remove the stigma from children by moving them out of adult courts and jails and treating them more like children in need of parental guidance. Advocates of expanded due process rights for juveniles want to protect children from arbitrary acts of the state. Irate citizens want protection from young offenders and call for harsher penalties. The court's early attempts to deny the child's offender status were unsuccessful because they failed to take into consideration the legitimacy of the community's desire for protection.

Yet, young offenders *are* significantly different from adult offenders. Youths are still learning about right and wrong and the community bears some responsibility for teaching them the difference. They have less firmly ingrained patterns of behavior than adults and therefore may be more amenable to change. Adolescents have a higher rate of misbehavior than other age groups, but they have a tendency to "age out" of delinquency as they get older (Murray and Cox, 1979; Farrington, Ohlin, and Wilson, 1986). Even though a small percentage of juvenile offenders commit a high percentage of the total number of juvenile offenses and those with more adjudications are more likely to offend again (Wolfgang, et al., 1972; Hamparian et al., 1978), we have no accurate way of predicting specifically who will continue to commit offenses and who will not (Lundman, 1984). Because of its continuing concern for the offender's child status, the juvenile court gives youths a chance to move out of offending behavior with minimal stigma. This is a very important role for the court that supports its physical separation from adult court.

Ideally, the court has the responsibility for meeting the needs of children in its care and for protecting the community from victimization. "When we stop worrying about whether our mandate is to provide custody or care and realize that our mission is to do both, we can begin to make progress," says Kay Murray, counsel to a large, urban pre-trial detention system for juveniles (1986). "There's absolutely no question. Our mandate is to provide custody. It is also to provide services, things the kids need. If they need to learn to read, we teach them; if they need glasses, we give them glasses; if they need counseling, we provide counselers." The justice system's responsibility for the children in its care is *not* the same as being responsible for all the children in the community who are having problems. It is this broader mandate, e.g., to help keep children out of trouble, that posed problems for the early juvenile court and raised serious questions about children's rights in the 1960s and 1970s.

A recent report on American attitudes toward crime and corrections suggests that there is strong public support for addressing the root causes of crime and for responding firmly and legally to juvenile offenders. Americans across the country who participated in a series of discussion groups designed to elicit attitudes about courts and corrections expressed a nearly unanimous belief that the underlying causes of crime result from a variety of social and economic factors related to growing up with poor living conditions, lack of education, and poor job opportunities (Doble and Rovner, 1986:22–23). Citizens were worried that unless these root causes were addressed, high crime would continue to plague our society. They also stressed that kids end up in trouble because the community fails to discourage their criminal activity and a main cause of crime is the lack of any real threat of punishment (1986:31–32). In other words, Americans feel it is important to respond to both the child status and the offender status. They want the community to address the root causes of a child's crime and the juvenile justice system to show youths that criminal activity carries negative consequences.

The court can do the latter and attempt to change the lives of children who come into its domain so they can function more competently, but it cannot address the root causes of crime. Only the community can do that. A realistic approach to juvenile courts that entails a clear commitment to both the child and offender statuses of youths who come into the juvenile justice system may help the court clarify its priorities and practices. An understanding that the court's range of activity has to be limited and that delinquency prevention is primarily the *community's* responsibility may help both communities and courts establish realistic expectations about their own and each other's objectives.

Need for A National Commitment to Children

The legal system, no matter how we organize it, cannot solve the problems of our children nor our ambivalence about adolescents. By the time many youths get to court, their life patterns are set and disability has compounded disability. Many lack basic skills like reading and writing. Many have been victims of abuse or neglect, and their families have provided few positive role models to guide them toward becoming responsible and independent adults. By adolescence, a substantial number will find themselves trapped in a seemingly endless cycle of community welfare, mental health programs, and medical and correctional services. In the past, we have expected the court to use its power to change difficult children and their parents. Against overwhelming odds, some judges, probation officers, and correction workers have succeeded. But the cost has been high and sometimes their better efforts have been at the expense of the court's legal goals. There is not much the court or its related agencies can do to "save" a child at 14 or 15. It is much harder to reform than to form. It is also expensive. A reform school costs approximately $30,000 a year per youth (Hechinger, 1986).

The role of the juvenile justice system could be clarified and strengthened if it operated within a comprehensive national policy for children and young adults similar to that in Sweden and other European countries. Today, the

United States is almost the only industrialized nation without such a consensus about its responsibility to its children. We are lulled by our own rhetoric. We accept the ideology of equal opportunity and do not see the gap in American society between that ideology and children's lives. Few of us realize, for example, the long-term implications of the fact that today over a fourth of all American children—half of all Black children—live below the poverty level (Julian and Kornblum, 1986:211).

How might a coherent national policy for children improve services for children and clarify the role of the juvenile justice system? First, such a policy would provide a consensus that children, all children, are entitled to a fair share of our nation's resources from the beginning of their lives. Sweden, for example, has adopted a family policy that stresses the importance of children being wanted, provides free prenatal and postnatal care, gives paid nine month paternity and maternity leave after a baby's birth, and provides extensive medical, social, and educational support services for *all* children and parents (O'Kelly and Carney, 1986).

It is important to begin this kind of commitment in the early stages of a child's life. We *know* what promotes the development of healthy, competent children and adults. We *know* how to make a difference in the lives of children. Research shows consistently that parental child-rearing practices and a child's poor educational achievement are among the best predictors of serious delinquency (Farrington, Ohlin, and Wilson, 1986). Yet, we have not agreed that the goal of comprehensive services for children and families is important enough to merit collective action designed to target resources or solve organizational problems.

A national policy for children begins with the need for early sex education and easy access to birth control. One baby in five and one of every two Black children are born to unmarried women (National Center for Health Statistics, 1985; Fuchs, 1983), most of them adolescents. In the past 15 years, the percentage of out-of-wedlock births in New York City nearly doubled, from 21 percent of all births in 1970 to 39 percent of all births in 1985. (Many of the fathers neither support nor acknowledge these children (Freedman, 1986).) It has been well-documented that single teenage mothers tend to have less education than other mothers, live below the poverty level, and, ultimately, have more children (Fuchs, 1983). Their babies do not have the same life chances as other babies in our society, and many subsequently turn up in juvenile court in abuse and neglect proceedings or on delinquency petitions.

We know that good physical care, reasonably consistent discipline, genuine affection and acceptance, concern for changing developmental needs, and cognitive stimulation help children grow into productive, competent adults.

For instance, Head Start programs in the 1960s and 1970s, which provided enriched, learning environments for children ages 3–6, yielded striking intellectual gains in preschool children. The loss of these gains as children moved into elementary school is less an indictment of Head Start than a symptom of the deadening effects of other environmental influences on children. Even with some losses, follow-up studies indicate that, in general, children in these programs had a higher rate of school success than similar children who were not in Head Start (Schweinhart and Weikart, 1980).

If we provided social and educational support to families with young children, perhaps adolescence would become less problematic. For families with difficult adolescents or families in crisis, the community can give special help. Intensive family-based programs, like Homebuilders in Washington and FAMILIES, Inc. in Iowa, are models of intensive support to families given by workers who devote several hours a week to just two or three families over a period of several weeks or months (Edna McConnell Clark Foundation, 1985).

On the other hand, some adolescents may need to separate themselves from difficult family situations (Mahoney, A., 1977). A recent study of runaways found that 46 percent of runaways had been forced from their homes or encouraged to leave by their parents. Thirty-nine percent gave physical abuse as one reason for leaving home and 26 percent mentioned sexual abuse. These findings suggest that family substitutes may be appropriate for some youths. If we could address difficult home situations when potential problems first come to the community's attention, we might be able to provide family support or alternatives to destructive home environments and thereby avoid subsequent, more serious, problems (Greenwood and Zimring, 1985). Because we equate juvenile offenders with children and maintain the belief that they should be kept at home, we are less innovative than we might be in developing alternative living arrangements for them outside the family. Residential work and educational programs, national service, and emancipation are all possibilities that have not yet been fully explored.

A comprehensive policy for children and young adults could develop programs that would provide opportunities for youths over a certain age to leave home and acquire the skills and experience needed to prepare them for decent jobs and the responsibilities of family life. Such programs could be voluntary, and would involve youths who had either parental approval or recommendations from school or social service workers. If such programs could include alternative school programs and a range of diagnostic and treatment services, youths with special problems such as alcohol or drug addiction, learning disabilities, or physical or emotional difficulties could be helped before their problems brought them into trouble with the law.

We can't achieve equal life chances for all children by assisting them at just one point in their lives. Head Start showed us that, and that realization may be one reason why we were disappointed with it. We had hoped for a magical solution, a three-year-concentrated educational program that would send children on their educational way without any further infusion of resources. A comprehensive policy for children entails attention to all stages of childhood in all environments in which children live, not just a one shot effort.

We are a wealthy country. We *can* devise a plan to promote the well-being of all children if we choose. A comprehensive plan for children's services would provide a framework for the juvenile court that should help it clarify its objectives and its position in the network of services.

Future Role of the Juvenile Court

It is not yet clear where the juvenile justice system is going. The court serves as a protector of the rights of children whenever they are individually or collectively at risk and is based on the premise of difference due to age. It also applies community standards of legal behavior to children and adolescents. It is a legal institution, not a social service agency, and it is set up specifically to handle the special needs and life circumstances of children and adolescents. These differences should guide the court's policy. Yet, some observers argue that the juvenile court has come to resemble so completely an adult criminal court that it is no longer needed (Feld, 1984; McNally, 1983). The argument probably will get stronger as resources continue to shrink and budgets become tighter. Opponents of the court may even seek to eliminate it quietly by transferring serious offenders into adult criminal courts and minor offenders into informal services or municipal courts. But before we let this happen, we need to reconsider the role of the juvenile court.

Evaluation research on delinquency prevention and control programs has given us empirical information about the effectiveness of a variety of approaches to delinquents (Lundman, 1984; Farrington, Ohlin, and Wilson, 1986). It provides a useful basis to evaluate and establish future court strategies. It suggests, moreover, that a graduated approach to juvenile offenders based on the number and seriousness of offenses might provide a useful framework for a coherent court policy. (The graduated approach is illustrated by Figure 8.1.) We have already discussed level 1, a national policy of support services for all children. Clarification about responsibility for this level of response is important. In the past, many delinquency prevention efforts have been associated with the court or court agencies, rather than a comprehensive program of services for all children.

**Figure
8.1**   **A graduated approach to juvenile offenders**

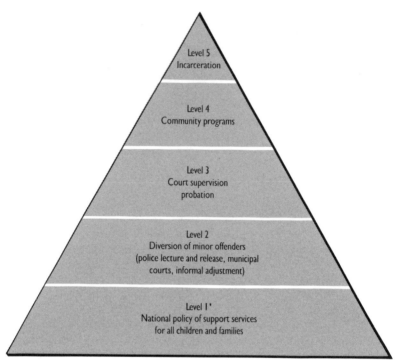

Level 5
Incarceration

Level 4
Community programs

Level 3
Court supervision
probation

Level 2
Diversion of minor offenders
(police lecture and release, municipal
courts, informal adjustment)

Level 1 *
National policy of support services
for all children and families

* This figure is not drawn to scale. The actual population of
children who never come into the court system is much larger than
the size of this band.

   Traditional prevention programs have attempted to identify youths headed
for trouble and tried to provide services to keep them out of trouble. There
is some disagreement about how successful these programs have been, but
research suggests generally that they have not done much to reduce delinquency
(Lundman, 1984). They also pose some problems in regard to invasion of
privacy and stigmatization of youths who have never been charged with an
offense. We do not know how to reliably identify individual juveniles headed
for trouble with the law and thus cannot justify either the cost of such measures
or their potential violation of the rights of juveniles and families singled out
for intervention efforts. The poor success and potential problems of prevention
programs support the case for putting prevention resources into a comprehensive program that is aimed at providing support services for all families
without consideration for delinquency potential. Thus, level 1 in our program
of response to troublesome and troubling children comes prior to court contact

and does not distinguish potentially delinquent children from other children. Its emphasis is on the well-being of all American children.

Level 2 responses, primarily to youths who begin to get in trouble with the law for minor offenses, attempt to divert youths away from court involvement through techniques such as police lecture and release; informal adjustment between youths, parents, and victims; municipal court fines; or voluntary referral to treatment centers. Although diversion combined with counseling has not been especially effective (Farrington, Ohlin, and Wilson, 1986), research on diversion programs indicates that diversion alone (without intervention) is effective, especially for minor offenders. We know that many adolescents engage in deviant and minor criminal behavior in their mid to late teens, but that a high percentage "age out" of this kind of behavior on their own. For most youths, some symbolic gesture to communicate that violation of the law is unacceptable may be sufficient to deter more serious delinquent behavior.

More severe responses are needed for youths who continue to clash with the law. Level 3 requires court acknowledgment of the offense and a period of probation. Previous research suggests that court supervision in the form of simple probation without other intervention is effective and relatively inexpensive for chronic property offenders (Lundman, 1984). A term of probation puts youths on notice that their behavior is not acceptable, is being monitored, and will be more severely sanctioned if it continues. Timely case processing is essential because many repeat offenders come from homes with inconsistent and indecisive child-rearing practices and have difficulty in connecting actions and consequences. Long delays between a youth's offense and court response minimize the impact of the court's action and further compound the negative effects of the youth's earlier home experiences.

At this stage, other service systems may be tapped in an effort to help youths with special needs. Does the family need help in parenting an adolescent? Does the youth have special educational or vocational needs? Is the youth a good candidate for emancipation, e.g., legal separation from parents, or recommendation to voluntary community based or residential educational or job training programs? Is the youth about to become a parent and in need of family support services from that perspective? If the court is operating within the context of a system of child and family services, these options can be explored without their being tied to the court or probation.

If a youth continues to get in trouble, the court moves to its level 4 response—nonvoluntary involvement in community programs that involve closer supervision. At level 4, the youth's needs are still paramount, but there is a shift toward increased concern for community protection. This level of services is least developed in many of our communities and most in need of our best creative, therapeutic, and organizational energies. It also requires close coordination between the court and the full range of services for youths and families. Many youths who require level 4 responses have a multitude of problems in addition to delinquency. Often they have had a series of foster care placements and been in and out of their own homes over several years on abuse and neglect petitions. As a result, they have never had an opportunity to form emotional attachments to other people. Many are well on their way to being multiple offenders by the age of 10. These children move quickly through levels 2 and 3 and pose the most serious challenge for the court and other childcare agencies. If we had viable level 1 programs, we might be able to reduce the number of these seriously troubled children. Until we do, however, we must bear the consequences of this deficiency and try to develop programs at levels 4 and 5 to help children learn the skills they need to function in society.

At earlier levels, responses here need to be timely and carry clear consequences. Well-supervised community work programs (with flexible working hours so youths can attend school) may be one set of alternatives that can be expanded. Another may be community centers like the Argus Learning for Living Center in the Bronx. "The key is bonding," says Elizabeth Sturz, its founder, "being incorporated into society, first at the program level and then into the larger community. Another key is self esteem. These are the essential ingredients, missing in the lives of high risk youths . . ." (Sturz, 1983:398). Level 4 programs are community based and, although some of them may be residential, they represent alternatives to incarceration. We should be aware, however, that successful community alternatives to incarceration are difficult to build (Smith, 1983–84).

At the top of the pyramid in Figure 8.1 is level 5, incarceration or transfer into adult criminal courts and correctional facilities, ideally necessary for only a very small percentage of youths—chronic offenders convicted of serious crimes of violence. Incarceration has been highly touted in the early 1980s as useful for incapacitating offenders, thereby protecting the community and reducing the number of overall offenses. However, the logic and statistical justification for this position is dubious (Mahoney A., 1986), and the long-term costs have not been adequately discussed. Institutional programs do not appear to be very effective in changing behavior and research shows that there is great continuity in offending and other deviant activities from childhood to adulthood (Farrington, Ohlin, and Wilson, 1986). Thus, incapacitation may yield short-term reductions in offense rates, but is not feasible as a long-term solution. Incarceration is expensive, possible for only relatively short periods of time and not very effective in changing behavior. Any long-term effort to reduce offense rates has to break the cycle of offending from adolescence to adulthood and from parent to child. Institutional treatment experiments do not look promising as a means for reducing recidivism, and we have little firm knowledge about the effects of imprisonment on the achievement of the basic objectives of the criminal justice system or on the prisoners while doing time and after release (Farrington, Ohlin, and Wilson, 1986). In light of this lack of knowledge, we should use incarceration only for our most dangerous youths.

The set of legal responses illustrated in Figure 8.1 follows a logical progression from primary consideration of the child to emphasis on community protection. We take our risks on the child's behalf in the early stages, but shift our emphasis to community protection as the youths convince us by their actions that they are a threat. The number of youths in each response band should drop sharply as we move up the triangle.

In order for this graduated approach to be effective, charges should accurately reflect a youth's behavior. Overcharging and plea bargaining to dismiss petitions or reduce charges make it harder for both the youth and court officials to see what response is appropriate. The emphasis should be less with the *number* of offenses than with their *type* and *severity*. Since the graduated approach is based on a youth's record, accurate information on prior records in other jurisdictions is important. In Suburban Court, a third of the youths lived outside Suburban County, and some had records in every court in the area even though they did not show up in official files. This lack of vital information made it extremely difficult for the court to respond appropriately to a youth.

Some form of this graduated approach to juvenile offenders is now used in most juvenile courts. But the response varies from jurisdiction to jurisdiction and from year to year depending on the existence of special programs, changes in legislation, and the success of agencies in their interorganizational negotiations for funds and clients. A substantial amount of the funds in many court systems go into diversion "programs" although research shows they are no more effective than diverting minor offenders from the formal court process altogether. The same is true for level 3 responses. Probation investigation and treatment services do not appear to yield much more success at this level than probation, e.g., putting a youth on notice that he or she better stay out of trouble over the next six months or a year.

If responses in the first three levels entail only minimal intervention in a youth's life, they may remain essentially prelegal and do not require full-blown legal handling. Resources now poured into large numbers of routine cases could be reserved for responses at levels four and five, where the youth *is* at risk for substantial court intervention and where community protection becomes an issue. The advantage of a graduated approach is that it establishes priorities at each level of offense severity and enables us to clearly identify when a youth's rights are at issue so that we can provide a full set of legal protections at that point. It also helps us set priorities in regard to deployment of resources and develop guidelines against which we can measure the objectives of proposed programs.

Suburban Court had a graduated approach to offenders, but it was not a clearly articulated policy that pervaded the entire court network. If it had been, the juvenile justice network would have been in a better position to understand the potential impact of several changes on its operation. It might have welcomed the entrance of the municipal courts into its arena and would have attempted to coordinate their efforts with the juvenile court's level 2 diversion program rather than viewing the municipal court as a competitor for clients. It also might have defined the PAC's role as an aggressive developer of level 4 programs and deemed the autonomous diagnostic team as unnecessary.

This study of Suburban Court shows that many factors influence a court's ability to fulfill its role besides its philosophy, and that juvenile courts desperately need management information and administrative support as they move from informal hearings to full-fledged legalistic courts. Suburban Court's problems were most acute in the middle range of cases with youths who had substantial records of property offenses and did not appear to be functioning well in the community, but who did not yet have a record for violence. Treatment facilities for these youths were less successfully developed in Suburban Court than other types of placement and probably are underdeveloped in other juvenile courts as well. Yet is it here that the need for treatment programs is greatest.

The legislation that reduced out-of-home placement targeted this range of programs for expansion. When it removed state restrictions that prohibited reimbursement for local expenditures on community programs, it took the first step toward developing innovative programs which would permit a graduated approach to young offenders. But the attempt had only limited success because there was no clear set of priorities and expectations for the overall court network. Organizations in the network approached this change as they approached all court changes, with an eye toward what they might gain or lose from it. The uneasy coalition of cost cutters and child advocates who passed the legislation carried their ambivalence and the ambivalence of the communities they represented into the implementation phase.

This book is about one effort to develop community alternatives by primarily manipulating the resource base to create financial incentives toward community programs. It shows how difficult this turned out to be and highlights some of the organizational, economic, and philosophic reasons why. Hopefully it also shows how we might do better next time.

Juvenile justice entails establishment of priorities, protection of rights, problem solving, and good management. Once we stop seeking magical solutions, we may begin to move more realistically and creatively toward a workable system of justice.

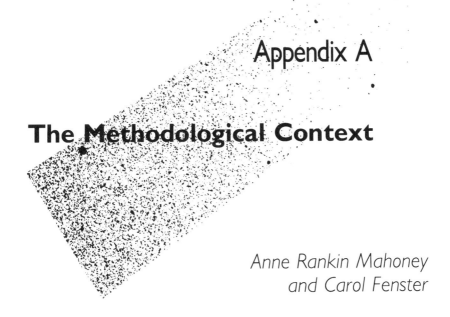

Appendix A

The Methodological Context

*Anne Rankin Mahoney
and Carol Fenster*

Researchers for the Suburban Youth Project utilized a wide range of sources —qualitative data from participant's observations, formal interviews with agency heads, informal discussions among staff members connected with the juvenile court; and newspaper articles chronicling important developments and issues in the county's juvenile justice network; and quantitative data from court records. A description of the researchers' roles in the court during field work gives some flavor of the nature of participant observation in a highly sensitive and political environment, and also gives a sense for the context of the research process.

Fieldwork in the Court

Context

The study of Suburban Court was one part of a research project, called the Suburban Youth Project, carried out from January 1, 1980 through June 30,

1982. The other part of the project involved the screening for giftedness of all youths who entered the system and agreed to be interviewed. Screening was carried out over a one-year period by project interviewers in three court agencies: the probation department, the juvenile diversion program, and the youth diagnostic team. Although their primary role was the identification of youths eligible for the giftedness portion of the research and the screening of youths for giftedness, these interviewers also worked (with the knowledge of the agencies) as observers for the court portion of the study. In order to identify and screen youths successfully, the interviewers had to be well integrated into the agencies in which they worked.

The approval of the juvenile judge was needed to begin the project; he signed a court order giving authorized staff members of the project access to court records. A series of meetings was held by top project personnel with the heads and staffs of key court agencies, both before the project started and as it progressed, to explain the goals and procedures of the research, answer questions, and respond to concerns. In all our actions we openly maintained the role of researcher, and introduced ourselves as members of the Suburban Youth Project, a research project connected with a local university. All agreements about research procedures were put in writing and signed by key research staff members and the agency heads involved. A great deal of staff energy initially was directed toward establishing field contacts at different points in the court network.

The probation department offered the project office space in its suite of offices in a building beside the courthouse. The office provided a central location for all researchers and further legitimated the research in the court environment. We worried at first that this tie with probation would bias our observations, but we became convinced as the project wore on that the advantages of having the office far outweighed the disadvantages. Probation workers were key figures in the court and their support and trust opened many doors. They made no effort, that we could see, to control us or our research. Because they worked with most of the agencies in the court network, they were invaluable sources of information on details of how the network really worked. Sometimes we found ourselves adopting their perspectives and we had to remain constantly aware that this was a problem. Our fight against a probation bias was made easier by workers in the other agencies in which we moved. They wanted to make sure we understood *their* perspective and were quick to tell us where we or probation were wrong.

Both parts of the project were dependent upon access to and the active cooperation of many staff members at all levels of the court network. Because acceptance was so crucial, the building and maintenance of ties with the judge, secretaries, staff workers, clerks, and the directors of agencies was an ongoing concern.

Gaining Acceptance in the Field

In general we were well received in the field and trusted with agency files, yearly reports, and personal insights volunteered by persons at all levels within the agencies. There were times when our acceptance seemed almost too easy and when we were not quite sure what to do with all the information we were getting.

Once the project was underway, there were other areas of adjustment. One involved the "intermeshing" of our researchers with several agencies, each of which had a different style of interaction. Each agency had a distinct personality, perhaps because of the professional and philosophical backgrounds of its staff. As a result, they had distinct ways of viewing problems and issues generated both from within and without. The accepted mode of interaction within one agency, for example, was one of joking, bantering, teasing, and a general "roll with the punches" attitude toward jobs and clients. Intragency tensions and disagreements were handled in the same manner. In contrast, the personality of another agency was solemn; they approached their jobs seriously and rarely joked.

In an organizational environment in which loyalties are important, ours were always under scrutiny. One of our most difficult tasks as we worked in agencies on a day-to-day basis was remaining impartial. This was especially difficult for our research assistants who usually had more contact with members of the agencies in which they worked than they did with other research staff members. Sometimes they got so caught up in the ethos of their organizations that they began to argue with each other in research staff meetings about the relative merits of their programs. These arguments were invaluable in highlighting different perspectives and helping us realize how difficult it was to keep a balanced perspective. Nevertheless, the maintenance of a neutral stance was a constant point of tension.

Our need to remain neutral kept us at a psychological distance from our agencies, and despite the relative ease with which we gained access and cooperation, we still felt like outsiders. This feeling was particularly acute for the field supervisor who also functioned as the court observer. She did not have a defined service role as the interviewers did, and she was not assigned to and integrated into any one agency. She moved throughout the system, not fitting anywhere, interacting with line staff and supervisory personnel in many organizations.

Sometimes the topic of discussion would rapidly change when the field supervisor entered a room. Sometimes it did not, and she wished it had as she tried to figure out what motivated workers to be so open in front of her. Did they trust her and her sense of loyalty and confidentiality? Did they not care if the information were passed on to others? Were they "staging" a conversation to allow her to gather information on topics too sensitive to be gathered directly?

As the agency staff members became more comfortable with our research staff, they also became more open about interagency conflicts. It got harder to remain neutral and cooperative with everybody. For example, one morning the juvenile probation supervisor and the prosecutor clashed bitterly in court over a disposition recommendation. The court observer was invited to join the probation staff for lunch that day, as she sometimes was, and animosity toward the district attorney dominated the luncheon conversation. The observer felt she had done a good job of maintaining neutrality during lunch and had avoided any direct opinion concerning the "rightness" or "wrongness" of the youth's disposition. She was, therefore, unprepared to find that the prosecutor was angry with her that afternoon. He made it clear that he considered her lunch with the probation department as an acceptance of its position in the dispute. The observer learned one of the cardinal rules of field work: Neutrality has a public as well as a private face. Field workers are always being observed, evaluated, and sometimes misinterpreted.

A related problem was the need to maintain confidences and not pass on information to members of one agency about what was going on in another agency. Often interviewers and observers were gently, or not so gently, encouraged to provide some insight into how another agency was handling a situation, or how the questioner was doing his or her job.

"Well, are we doing a good job?" was a question all researchers on the project fielded regularly. To help our field workers remain neutral and keep confidences, we maintained strong guidelines about not sharing information and often reminded our own staff as well as workers in the system about our commitment to confidentiality regarding children and staff members.

Our general acceptance in Suburban Court is an important dimension of this research. We believe that one reason we were accepted was because we directed our attention to structure and process rather than to personalities. We came to feel early in our research that individuals and agencies in Suburban Court genuinely cared about children and wanted to do a good job. They knew that the system, like all court systems, had problems. They were frustrated in their attempts to work constructively with juveniles and wanted to see improvements in finding ways to help troubled children.

Courtroom Observations

All court observations took place in the primary juvenile courtroom where cases were handled by one full-time judge. We usually observed on Tuesdays and Thursdays, when most delinquency cases were handled. The court observer sat in court occasionally on other days to get a better understanding of the full range of the work of the juvenile judge, and on occasions when cases of particular interest to the research were being heard.

Observations were usually done by the same person because early in the research it became clear that continuity in interaction was important. The potential bias of one observer was mitigated by the perspectives of observers in other parts of the system, joint interviews with key personnel during the two years of data collection, and the quantitative court record data. We also checked the observer's perceptions by occasionally having a second observer sit in court or having someone else replace her.

The juvenile courtroom is small with limited seating in an area designed for jurors. The observer sat in this section along with probation officers, social services workers, and other agency personnel with business in the court, as well as family members or others interested in the case.

Each day the bailiff gave the observer the day's docket, which helped her keep track of youths as they came into court and provided an indicator of the size of the day's calendar. If she missed a day, he saved the docket for her. Hearings were scheduled to begin at 8:30 A.M. but usually got started around 9:00. This half hour was a particularly fruitful time for observation. The observer would usually station herself in the waiting room adjacent to the courtroom in order to watch youths and their families check in, interact with the bailiff, and listen to and participate in conversations between courtroom officials. Sometimes these conversations were frivolous, joke-telling sessions. Other times they were serious discussions about what to do with a youth, the options available to the court, and the likelihood of a child successfully completing treatment goals. She also overheard conversations between youths and their parents in the waiting room. These episodes provided some understanding of how families perceived the court experience.

Courtroom observations provided an understanding of day-to-day operations of the court and its staff and yielded ideas about what information to look for in the official records. It also sensitized us to the complex interaction patterns and unwritten expectations of court participants, and provided information about individual cases that was not obtainable from court records.

Despite the eclectic nature of this portion of the project, there were several types of information that the observer collected regularly. She routinely noted comments participants made about the factors they considered in making treatment decisions; the appearance, demeanor, and interactions of youths and their families; persons accompanying the youth to hearings; and interactions between courtroom officials. For each case, the observer also noted who was involved, the offense, the youth's age and sex, and the outcome of the hearing. She tried to chronicle the sequence of events leading up to the recorded situation or episode as well as its outcome.

There was always at least one probation counselor seated near the observer and this gave her the opportunity to discuss cases between hearings, note the reactions of probation officers to cases, and witness their interactions with youths and other courtroom officials. The observer came to be quite familiar with the probation counselor's routine (that is, recording the hearing's outcome and other important notations on the youth's file). The counselors came to accept her so much that they sometimes handed her a stack of files and asked her to "carry on" for them while they took a few minutes to hold an impromptu conference with a youth.

The court is the arena in which all actions involving delinquents eventually are legitimated. In the course of the year, the observer came to know by name and face almost everyone in the county who was directly involved with it. She became part of the courtroom scene, blending in easily with other agency personnel who also entered the court with files and clipboards and took notes. She came to be included, as a matter of course, in the banter that was carried on among the judge, bailiff, clerk, stenographer, district attorney, and probation officers.

With the judge's permission, the observer took detailed notes during court proceedings. Here, as elsewhere in the research, confidentiality and neutrality were carefully maintained. The observer never used names in her notes, recording only the titles of the courtroom actors or the youths' case numbers. In addition, she was careful about what she wrote in the courtroom itself, often resorting to short phrases or key words to denote certain episodes, which she wrote up in detail back in the office. She often used the docket sheet to cover up her notes when she wasn't writing, especially when she was recording sensitive events or statements.

At the end of each observation session, or at least on the same day, the observer transcribed her notes into complete sentences and paragraphs, utilizing topic headings for each episode so we could refer to the event later on. When fully transcribed and typed, the notes were filed in the project office at the university. No notes were ever kept in the field office in the Court Services Building. During the year, the project amassed several hundred pages of notes about interaction between courtroom participants and the children and families that came before the court. These observations provide rich background data for the quantitative analysis of official records and were helpful in developing the codebooks and coding.

Agency Observations

The interviewers who conducted the screening and assessment for giftedness carried out their interviewing in three different court agencies—juvenile probation, the district attorney's juvenile diversion program, and the youth diagnostic team. All three agencies insisted, at least initially, that the project interviewers integrate themselves into their host agencies so that they understood the general philosophy and procedures of the agency and could work well within it. This integration also enabled them to do observation for the case study part of the research for which they were trained early in the project. Their dual role was made clear to agencies from the beginning of the research project's contact with them.

The interviewers attended agency staff meetings, sometimes participated in treatment or evaluation activities for which they were qualified, and essentially "lived" in their agencies as staff members. Their attendance at meetings provided a sense of the day-to-day problems faced by each agency, their manner of coping with them, and their own perceptions of their place in the court network. Absorption of our research assistants by their host agencies was so complete it became a problem. One was actually mentioned by his co-workers as a candidate for the job of temporary director of his program when the full-time director left to take another job.

Maintaining neutrality was an ongoing problem. Competition existed between the east side branch and the west side branch in both probation and diversion. Sometimes our staff members, who attended meetings of both branches, were pumped by workers in one office for information about what was going on in the other office. Neutrality was also a problem in dealing with several agencies simultaneously. There was always at least one agency that was "scorned" by the others. The reason for the scorn varied. Sometimes it was because an agency decided to modify its procedures in such a way that it could cause more work for another agency. At other times, the reason was disagreement over what treatment a child needed. One never knew which agency would be on the "scorn" list, and the scorned agency was sure to be discussed in uncomplimentary ways. During these discussions, it was difficult to avoid being drawn in. Sometimes agency members deliberately baited researchers to try to elicit an opinion.

Another problem that interviewers and observers felt acutely was that agency members were never quite certain when the researchers were "on" or "off," (e.g., when they were collecting data or just being themselves). As research assistants became better acquainted with agency workers, conversations turned often to personal topics like free time activities, vacations, and opinions. Even then researchers were sometimes asked if they were taking notes, even though the conversation had nothing to do with juvenile justice.

Interagency Observations

The primary site for observation of interagency action was the Placement Alternatives Commission (PAC). It includes representatives from several agencies serving juveniles in the county. A project observer attended PAC meetings regularly during 1980 and most of 1981. The observer initially made contact with the Commission when she and other project personnel met with it to acquaint its members with the research project and to seek permission to place an interviewer in the diagnostic team, which was under its authority. Commission members invited project staff members to return at any time and indicated that PAC meetings were open to the public. Shortly after the Suburban Court research got underway in 1980, a project observer began to attend the weekly meetings in a nonparticipating role.

Observing PAC meetings provided insights into the interorganizational dimension of the court network. Information we obtained there often made sense of observations or tensions elsewhere in the network that we hadn't been able to understand. They also laid bare the roles of organizations which were important to the court but rarely appeared there. The directors of the two mental health centers in the county attended PAC meetings and played an important role in decisions that directly effected the juvenile court. We would not have been aware of their influence if we had not attended PAC meetings on a regular basis. Nor would we have been as cognizant of the crucial role the department of social services plays in decisions about treatment services.

The PAC was the place where interorganizational dynamics could be identified and observed. Here, as nowhere else, one could sense the tensions between agencies, the territorial and power struggles, the personality conflicts. Observation yielded information and insights that helped make sense of what had happened elsewhere in the system and what was about to happen. It helped us to see that often participants themselves didn't understand or know about legislative and policy changes and gave rise to our interest in the possibility of an overload of change in a system.

In the meetings of the Placement Alternatives Commission we got a sense of how much went on under the surface that we would never be able to tap as researchers—the phone calls, hallway discussions, unspoken understandings, and fundamental disagreements. Observing PAC meetings provided a framework in which to view much of what we saw in the court network. It also made us humble, because it gave us some sense of how much we were missing and would always miss, regardless of whether we were insiders or outsiders.

PAC meetings yielded two kinds of data—actual observation notes by the observer and minutes and handouts distributed at meetings. The latter include budgets, local plans for reduction of out-of-home placement, population figures, and memos written by members of the commission. Minutes, relevant handouts, and observation notes are all included in the full set of research project field notes.

Interviews

In an effort to get answers to questions about certain kinds of cases appearing in court, new procedures instituted by agencies, or judicial decisions project staff members informally interviewed several agency workers (e.g., probation counselors, diversion counselors, supervisors of both agencies, court clerks, bailiffs) throughout the project. During the final six months of 1981, researchers also assembled a formal set of open-ended questions for a former juvenile judge, a newly appointed juvenile judge, a former probation worker, the chief probation officer, the district attorney in charge of the juvenile division, and the juvenile probation supervisor. These interviews provided a perspective on the juvenile justice network from the supervisory or administrative level and gave us a chance to fill in information gaps that had become apparent during preliminary analysis.

A series of taped interviews was also conducted with a probation officer who had been in the system for several years. We prepared sets of questions for him on a variety of topics, to which he taped answers at his own convenience. The tapes were then transcribed and added to the project field notes.

Organization of Field Materials

As the volume of field materials grew, they became more difficult to keep track of and gain access to. Initially, they were filed in different places. All court observations were together in one place; all notes from the Placement Alternatives Commission were together somewhere else. Some materials on the court agencies were with the test materials for the giftedness portion of the research. As the files grew, we felt as if we were drowning in a sea of paper. We could remember reading something, but couldn't remember which of the overlapping files it was in. As our need for having one agency's materials all together decreased, we broke apart the individual agency files and reorganized them into two separate sets of materials. One included all the materials on the methodology and mechanics of testing youths for giftedness. The other, the one relevant to the research described in this book, included all materials about the court and its agencies. We put everything—observations, interviews, minutes, agency reports, miscellaneous documents—in chronological order, and numbered the pages.

This chronological record has proved to be invaluable. For topics of particular interest we developed an index of relevant references by scanning through the materials, a tedious task but fascinating in its own right. With the index we were able to follow the activities of an agency or variations on a theme over the course of the two years covered by the materials. The materials did not provide a complete record of any one agency or topic, but provided a working framework.

Newspaper clippings were handled in a similar manner. All clippings were copied and two files were kept. One was chronological, a companion to the data volume, indexed in the same way and the pages numbered, identified in the text with the prefix N. The other was topical and clippings were dispersed into files on individual topics.

Part of the excitement of writing this book has come from following themes and incidents chronologically through the field materials, seeing the same event as viewed by different actors and from different organizational perspectives.

As we began to put together field materials for this book, we became concerned about how to protect the anonymity of the court and its participants, while at the same time maintaining scientific standards of reference and data citation. The way we resolved this problem was to cite pages in our chronological files of field notes and newspaper clippings simply by number without giving names of sources. Individuals are protected, but the necessary information on the sources is easily accessible if we need it.

If we were doing a field project again, we would start this chronological document at the beginning of the study, building it simultaneously with the files on separate agencies and topics. As we went along we could copy materials and develop a preliminary index. We also would include more materials on individual agencies such as annual reports, budgets, and guidelines on procedures.

Official Records

The types of official records utilized for this study include the files kept by the Clerk of the Court on each youth whose petition was filed in Juvenile Court during 1980; the files kept by the juvenile diversion program on each youth referred to that program during 1980; and annual reports kept by these two agencies of the Juvenile Court as well as those kept by the District Attorney's Office, the Department of Social Services, and commissions appointed to monitor the county's juvenile justice system.

The year 1980 was selected as the year for data collection from official records because it was the most current year available that would allow enough time for most cases to reach completion before the end of the research project. Also, 1980 was the year in which most of the court observation was done, thus providing an additional source of information on many of the cases in the quantitative study. A further reason for the choice of 1980 was that there were no significant legislative changes scheduled to go into effect during the year.

Juvenile Court Records

In early 1981, a preliminary version of the court records codebook was devised after hours of study of the court files. After an early version of the codebook was pretested on a random sample of cases, a final version was completed. The 17-page codebook includes 115 variables on the incidence of delinquency across the county by census tracts and municipalities, the family situation of youths, how these youths are processed through the Juvenile Court, characteristics of the delinquent act, and the factors affecting their dispositions. Of particular interest was the length of time that juvenile cases take to move from apprehension through disposition. Three coders were trained by the field supervisor and a high degree of reliability was established among the them.

In general, the juvenile court records tended to be complete, accurate, and easy to understand. The typical juvenile case file contained a copy of the petition(s) filed against the youth, the minute orders of each hearing including the hearing data, persons in attendance, what happened at the hearing, the judge's dispositional decision, and any other relevant documents such as a copy of the dismissal, the pre-dispositional report made by the probation counselor, and the bail release form.

Access to these juvenile court records was made possible by the court order given to research staff members at the beginning of the project by the juvenile judge. Since the police reports for all juvenile cases were stored in the

District Attorney's office rather than with juvenile court records, an additional court order from the judge plus the district attorney's permission was required to gain access to them. Access to the diversion records required written permission from the diversion director and the district attorney.

Every delinquency case filed in 1980 was coded, regardless of whether or not the youth resided in the court's jurisdiction. A list of all youths whose petitions were filed in the Juvenile Court was obtained from the probation department logs, which are considered to be highly accurate by court and probation personnel.

These cases are recorded on the logs by consecutive case number by year (e.g., 80JV0001, 80JV0002, etc.) and include the youth's name, number, age, petition filing date, residence, referral source (the police department who apprehended the youth), and the allegations. Using this list, the coders were able to locate each youth's file among cases in the office of the Clerk of the Court. As a final check to make sure all 1980 delinquency cases were included, coders pulled every 1980 juvenile case to see if it involved delinquency charges.

As the coding of the court records progressed, the coders kept track of which cases had already been coded by placing a checkmark beside the youth's name. A list was made of uncoded cases that could not be located or had not reached final disposition, and in August 1981 coders undertook a final search for uncoded cases, accounting for everyone.

Despite the relative accuracy and completeness of the juvenile case files, the coders were faced with several minor problems. One of these was the lag time between court hearings and the microfilming of records of nonresident youths whose files were returned to their home courts (change of venue). We needed the microfilm in order to code the case, but often had to wait several months to locate it because at the time of coding, the clerks in the microfilm department were approximately four months behind.

Another problem involved cases transferred from another county *into* Suburban county, either for disposition or continuation of supervision or probation. Because the courtroom procedures and record-keeping policies of these counties differed from Suburban county, the coders often had difficulty in understanding what had transpired in the previous court. Furthermore, these transferred cases rarely included police reports so it was hard to evaluate the severity of the youth's delinquent act and the circumstances surrounding it. During the coding process, the coders had the opportunity to review files from several surrounding counties in the metro area. They unanimously agreed that the files in Suburban county were superior to the files of other counties in regard to quality, accuracy, and completeness.

A final, though also relatively infrequent, problem involved minor inconsistencies, omissions, or errors made in recording the action in appearances. When these problems occurred, the coders' familiarity with courtroom procedures enabled them to sort out the facts. Because the staff was so well steeped in the system of Suburban county, coders were usually able to decipher confusing, inconsistent, or incomplete records.

The speed with which files could be coded varied considerably. Some files were very simple, straightforward, and easy to code. These files, once located, took approximately five minutes to complete. Others required considerably more time. These included files with more than one petition, several hearings, a pre-disposition report, and other miscellaneous sources of information. It was not unusual to spend 30 minutes on these "fat" files. Extremely complicated ones required an hour or more. This variation among cases made it difficult to estimate how much time was needed to complete the entire coding process. Logs kept by the coders show that the numbers of files coded in any one day varied depending on whether they drew simple or complex ones.

The coders adopted uniform policies in coding charges and prior records and in consolidating several cases involving the same youth. If a youth was charged with several delinquent acts, the most serious charge was coded. However, when measuring the amount of time required to process cases, the youth's *first* delinquent act was used (regardless of whether it was the most serious or not) so as to measure accurately the amount of time transpiring between a child's first apprehension and later decision points in the juvenile justice system.

A uniform method of consolidating several cases involving the same youth was adopted. Identification numbers for petitions were assigned consecutively during the calendar year starting with one. However, many youths had more than one petition filed against them during the year. During 1980, the court assigned an identification number for each new petition and then usually added the new petition to earlier petitions still pending against the youth and filed all the youth's petitions under the youth's first identification number. The court didn't catch all the multiple cases, however, and occasionally one youth would have several cases and several files. Sometimes the clerk picked this up and flagged the problem by noting on the folder(s) the other numbers assigned to the youth and under which JV number the case was being officially processed. A few youths with multiple petitions went unnoticed and were discovered when we assigned research identification numbers by name. We consolidated these few cases, coding earlier petitions as part of a youth's prior record. Our efforts to use the individual rather than the case as the unit of analysis highlighted some problems with court record studies.

It is clear that a substantial minority of youths have several petitions pending at once. Sometimes these multiple cases may be known to the court; sometimes they may not be. Sometimes the court's knowledge is noted on the record; sometimes it is not. Court records have social meaning that may not be apparent in anything written down. For example, several relatively minor cases take on different meanings depending on whether they are perceived by the court as involving only one youth or several different youths. Those different meanings may influence outcomes, but may never be articulated in writing in a file.

Case processing time may vary also, depending on whether the unit of analysis is a case or an individual. For example, one individual may have four cases pending at the same time. The first case takes 100 days to move from petition to final disposition. While it is in progress, the youth goes on a shoplifting binge and three more cases are filed: taking 44 days, 30 days, and 30 days. The mean number of days for the four cases is 51 days. However, the three shorter cases are consolidated into the one longer case. The time it takes that individual to resolve the four cases is 100 days, and in the calculation of means based on individuals, it is the 100-day case that is calculated in, not the shorter ones. Thus the calculation of processing time in a population based on *individuals* may show longer times than calculation based on a population of *cases*.

Diversion Record Study

The development of the codebook and coding procedures for cases processed by the juvenile diversion program are parallel to those for the coding of court records. After the bugs had been worked out of the court record coding, the codebook was modified for use with the diversion records, with an eye to adapting it to allow analysts to compare diversion and court populations on as many variables as possible, as well as to provide an independent picture of the diversion population.

A list of all youths whose cases were referred by the District Attorney to the Diversion Program was obtained from the Diversion secretary. This list contained the names of the youths and their diversion number (assigned in numerical order during a calendar year as the cases were received from the District Attorney)—(e.g., 001–80, 002–80, etc.). Youths were referred on either a voluntary or mandatory basis. We included only mandatory referrals in our study, those upon whom petitions would be filed if they did not enter diversion.

The population of coded diversion cases includes 452 youths, both residents and nonresidents of the county. The total includes 130 youths who were referred to diversion but were subsequently returned to the District Attorney for court filing. These youths failed to appear for their intake interview, denied the charges, rejected diversion and elected court handling, or were otherwise uncooperative. These "returned" youths were included in the population of 452 but were separated out for most analyses.

Diversion records include police reports, so both diversion and police information could be gathered on a case at the same time. The coding of diversion records went more slowly than had been anticipated. The most important parts of the records, the counselors' summaries of meetings and phone calls with their clients, were all handwritten. Deciphering these notes was difficult and time-consuming and occasionally the coders had to go directly to the counselor involved to seek clarification of material.

Coders followed a procedure similar to their procedure in coding court records in their efforts to ensure that all 1980 cases were located and coded. Their task was easier in diversion because there was almost no time lag between a child's referral and the commencement of his six-month treatment period. As a result there were no pending cases in diversion at the end of the coding period.

The quantitative and qualitative aspects of the research complemented each other in many ways. The field research enabled us to get some sense for the social meaning of records we coded. Our coding operations and the questions they raised added dimensions to our understanding of how the court worked.

Appendix B

Notes

Chapter I   The Juvenile Justice Network

1. The court has been given a pseudonym to help protect the anonymity of both children and staff. In a further effort to protect the research subjects, interviews, observations, memoranda, and agency reports used in the research are included in several volumes of field notes, entitled Suburban Youth Project (SYP) or Suburban Youth Project Newspaper Files (SYPN) and are cited here by their page numbers within those volumes. Anyone interested in seeing these original documents can do so by contacting the author.

2. The model is sometimes referred to as a resource dependence model (Pfeffer and Salancik, 1978; Scott, 1981), political economy model (Benson, 1975; Wamsley and Zald, 1973; Zald, 1970), or dependency exchange model (Hasenfeld, 1972; Jacobs, 1974; Thompson, 1967). It takes into account what Emerson (1983) calls "holistic concerns and influences," and

is compatible with the new paradigm shifts in organizational theory described by Schwartz and Ogilvy (1979) and Lincoln (1985). The new paradigms allow for the existence of multiple and mutual causality, and multiple orders.

3. The percentage of the population under 18 years of age *decreased* from 34.3 percent of the U.S. population in 1970 to 27 percent in 1982 to an estimated 23 percent in 2000. In contrast the percentage of the population 65 and over *increased* from 10 percent of the population in 1970 to 12 percent in 1982 to an estimated 13 percent in 2000. The number of persons 85 years of age and older, now about 1 percent of the population, is expected to double from 2.4 million in 1982 to 4.9 million by 2000 (Spencer, 1984:8).

Chapter 2   Dreams Over Time

1. Pound (1944:4–5) notes that the court came into existence in an era when men looked forward to a time when government would disappear, when governments were being remanded into a secondary and subordinate place and men would come to rely for order, safety, property and happiness simply on themselves.

Chapter 3   A Court in Its Context

1. The National Assessment of Juvenile Corrections, as part of its study of juvenile justice in the United States, undertook an examination and analysis of juvenile codes and related statutes. It reported that more than two-thirds of the states had passed major modifications in their Juvenile Codes between 1969 and 1972 (Levin and Sarri, 1974).

2. A total of 1,586 cases came to the District Attorney's attention in 1980, 98 of which were refused for reasons such as action by other agencies, insufficient evidence, or insufficient investigations by police. Of the remaining 1,488 requested petitions, the District Attorney actually filed 906 delinquency petitions. It is possible to account specifically for 835 of these. There are 710 youths in the 1980 court record study. Of these, many had additional petitions filed on them *before* they were adjudicated. Accordingly, 500 had 1 petition, 78 had 2 petitions, 15 had 3 petitions, 4 had 4 petitions and 1 had 6 petitions. There were 62 youths for whom there was no information on number of petitions. In addition to the 835

petitions, some petitions were added to the files of youths *after* adjudication. Also, other petitions may have been added to the files of youths whose cases had originated in 1979 and therefore would not have been picked up in our review of 1980 files. The rest of the cases were referred to the juvenile diversion program. Of those referred to diversion, 452 were eligible for inclusion in the study of 1980 diversion records. The remaining youths were not eligible because their participation in the diversion program was voluntary and there was not sufficient information on them in the files; they were referred to other agencies for official action; they were too old (over 18); or they moved from the jurisdiction after the referral was made. Only 322 youths remained in diversion. The other 130 were ultimately referred back to the prosecutor and presumably became part of the population of 710 youths upon whom petitions were filed.

3. Court statistics were computed in 1980 on the basis of the number of *petititions* filed in the court. Our study of court records was based on the number of *youths* who entered the court. A substantial number of youths had several petitions filed on them. Because our unit of analysis was the individual, and the court's practice was to handle all the petitions together, we consolidated all petitions involving one youth and counted them as one case. We counted prior petitions as part of a youth's previous record and had an elaborate coding scheme to handle the many permutations these complex cases created.

4. It was not possible to trace each case rejected by the diversion program to learn what decision the prosecutor finally made about it. We assume that most of the youths had petitions filed on them. It is possible that a few did not. The diversion records of youths whose cases were returned to the prosecutor showed the following reasons for return:

did not respond for intake	25
denied charges	16
unwilling to participate	27
unable to contact	14
pending charges	22
currently on probation	05
other	21
Total	130

5. Numerous researchers have found an association between marital discord and breakdown and an increased risk of delinquency (e.g., Rutter 1971; West and Farrington 1973).

6. The proclivity of Suburban Court youths toward theft and burglary offenses and the relatively small percentage of offenses against the person are similar to the pattern for youths nationally. *Uniform Crime Reports, 1982* (Federal Bureau of Investigation, 1983:176) shows that, of youths arrested for index offenses, 56 percent were arrested for larceny-theft and 26 percent for burglary. Slightly over 11 percent total were arrested for aggravated assault, robbery, forcible rape, or murder.

Chapter 4   Time-Bound Decisions

1. In this study we use means (averages), medians, and third quartile cases to describe case processing time for different phases of the process and different categories of cases. The *mean* permits statistical comparison of mean processing times for defendants with different characteristics or different kinds of cases. However, because means can be influenced by a handful of unusually long or short cases, it is also instructive to look at the *median*, which tells us how long it takes the middle case to move through the process. The *third quartile case* represents the disposition time for a case that takes longer than 75% of the cases in the population and less time than 25%, and indicates how long the slower cases in court take to be disposed of (Church et al., 1978a).

2. One stage, filing to adjudication, includes within it two shorter segments, filing to advisement and advisement to adjudication. We include figures for filing to adjudication because this is the period usually covered by time standards. Figures for the two shorter segments are useful, however, because they help identify where the bottlenecks are.

3. Our practice of combining all cases involving a specific youth would be expected to yield a somewhat longer case processing time for the whole package of cases than that recorded for each case individually.

4. Half of these 400 dispositions involved reserved adjudications, which often include adjudication and sentence together in the same hearing. The number of cases included in the analysis of the disposition population is roughly 250 to 300 less than the number in the analysis of other stages of the court process, because of the exclusion of dismissed, change of venue, and pending cases which did not receive a sentence in Suburban Court. Some of the cases included in the adjudication category, but not the disposition category, remained in the system for many months before they were adjudicated, and then were dropped out of the system. Thus they increased mean time in the stages between filing and adjudication,

but not mean time in the stages between filing and disposition. For   153
example, the range of time from filing to adjudication was 0 to 784 days,
the range of time from filing to disposition was 0 to 488 days.

Chapter 5   Constraints on Court Autonomy

1. The state was not alone in its reliance on out-of-state placements. Pro-
    ponents for interstate placement argue that they are often necessary to
    match a child's needs for care with the best services available. Hall,
    Principal Investigator of the Out-of-State Placement of Children Study
    at the Academy for Contemporary Problems in Columbus, Ohio sug-
    gests that a significant number of children throughout the country are
    placed outside their home states each year (1981:3). Exact numbers are
    hard to obtain. A Children's Defense Fund Study in 1976 reported that
    welfare officials in eight states reported that they did not know how
    many of their children were in facilities outside the state. Many more
    showed figures that were often inconsistent with those reported by the
    states to which they sent their children. The practice goes back to the
    child saving movement of the late 1800s when the New York Children's
    Aid Society placed over 90,000 children from New York slums in "good
    Christian homes around the country." (Hall, 1981:3) Criticisms of in-
    terstate placement center on the geographic separation of child and fam-
    ily, the difficulty in adequately monitoring the quality of care and
    systematically reviewing progress, as well as the greater cost (Allen and
    Knitzer, 1981:17–20).

2. This is the case in many jurisdictions across the country. Behar discusses
    the greater availability of reimbursement for costs of children in resi-
    dential care and the lack of payment for services to a child's family and
    for consultation with community agencies (1981:57–59).

Bibliography

Cases

U.S. vs. Furey. 500 F.2d 338 (1974).

Breed v. Jones. 421 U.S. 519, 95 S.Ct. (1975).

In re Gault. 387 U.S. 1, 18L Ed. 2nd 527, 87 S.Ct. 1428 (1967).

Kent v. U.S. 383 U.S. 541, 86 S. Ct. 1045 (1966).

McKeiver v. Pennsylvania. 403 U.S. 528, 91 S. Ct. (1971).

In re Winship. 397 U.S. 358, 90 S. Ct. 1068 (1970).

Statutes, Codes, and Standards

American Bar Association. National Conference of State Trial Judges. *Standards Relating to Court Delay Reduction*. Chicago: American Bar Association Press, 1984.

Conference of State Court Administrators. *National Time Standards for Case Processing*. Membership Meeting, Savannah, Georgia. Adopted July 1983.

Florida Rule of Juvenile Procedure 8.180(a) (1981).

Institute of Judicial Administration and American Bar Association. *Juvenile Justice Standards: Standards Relating to Court Organization and Administration*. Cambridge, Mass.: Ballinger, 1980a.

————. *Juvenile Justice Standards: Standards Relating to Adjudication*. Cambridge, Mass.: Ballinger, 1980b.

————. *Juvenile Justice Standards: Standards Related to Pretrial Court Proceedings*. Cambridge, Mass.: Ballinger, 1980c.

National Conference of State Trial Judges. *Standards Relating to Case Flow*

156   *Management and Time Delay Reduction.* Adopted by the ABA House of Delegates, August 1984.

Office of Juvenile Justice and Delinquency Prevention, National Advisory Committee for Juvenile Justice and Delinquency Prevention. *Standards for the Administration of Juvenile Justice.* Washington, D.C.: U.S. Government Printing Office, 1980.

Speedy Trial Act of 1974 18 USC s3161–74 (1976).

References

Aiken, Michael, and Jerald Hage. "Organizational Interdependence and Intra-organizational Structure." *American Sociological Review* (1968): 912–930.

Aldrich, Howard E., and Jeffrey Pfeffer. "Environments of Organizations." *Annual Review of Sociology* 2(1976): 79–105.

Allen, Francis A. *The Borderland of Criminal Justice*. Chicago: University of Chicago Press, 1964.

Allen, Mary Lee, and Jane Knitzer. "Out-of-Home Care: The Interstate Placement Experience." In *Major Issues in Juvenile Justice Information and Training: Readings in Public Policy*, edited by John C. Hall, Donna Martin Hamparian, John M. Pettibone, and Joseph L. White. Columbus, Ohio: Academy for Contemporary Problems, 1981, 9–32.

Bacharach, Samuel B., and Edward Lawler. *Power and Politics in Organizations*. San Francisco: Jossey-Bass Publishers, 1980.

Bardach, Eugene. *The Implementation Game: What Happens After a Bill Becomes a Law*. Cambridge, Mass.: MIT Press, 1977.

Baum, Lawrence. "Implementation of Judicial Decisions: An Organizational Analysis." *American Politics Quarterly* 1(1976).

Baum, Martha, and Stanton Wheeler. "Becoming an Inmate." In *Controlling Delinquents*, edited by Stanton Wheeler. New York: John Wiley, 1968.

Behar, Lenore B. "Serving Emotionally and Behaviorally Disturbed Children through Interstate Placement: An Unwritten Policy." In *Major Issues in Juvenile Justice Information and Training: Readings in Public Policy*, edited by John C. Hall, Donna Martin Hamparian, John M. Pettibone, and Joseph L. White. Columbus, Ohio: Academy for Contemporary Problems, 1981, 49–69.

Benson, J. Kenneth. "The Interorganizational Network as a Political Economy." *Administrative Science Quarterly* 20(1975): 229–249.

158   Blau, Peter M., and W. Richard Scott. *Formal Organizations*. San Francisco: Chandler, 1962.

Bortner, M. A. *Inside a Juvenile Court: The Tarnished Ideal of Individualized Justice*. New York: New York University Press, 1982.

Bozinovski, Susanna, and Carol Fenster. "Census Tract Characteristics and Policing Practices as Factors in High Delinquency Rates in a Suburban County." Unpublished paper presented to the Western Social Science Association annual meetings, Albuquerque, N.M., 1983.

Carey, James T., and Patrick D. McAnany. *Introduction to Juvenile Delinquency*. Englewood Cliffs, N.J.: Prentice-Hall, 1984.

Carter, Robert M., and Joseph D. Lohman. *Middle Class Delinquency: An Experiment in Community Control*. Berkeley: University of California, 1968.

Chance, Paul. "Adolescence: No Place Like Home." *Psychology Today* 20 (December, 1986): 12.

Children's Defense Fund (CDF). *Children Without Homes: An Examination of Public Responsibility to Children in Out-of-Home Care*. Washington, D.C.: 1978.

Church, Thomas W., Jr., Alan Carlson, Jo-Lynne Lee, and Teresa Tan. *Justice Delayed: The Pace of Litigation in Urban Trial Courts*. Williamsburg, Va.: National Center for State Courts, 1978a.

Church, Thomas W., Jr., Jo-Lynne Lee, Teresa Tan, Alan Carlson, and Virginia McConnel. *Pretrial Delay: A Review and Bibliography*. Williamsburg, Va.: National Center for State Courts, 1978b.

Cicourel, Aaron. *The Social Organization of Juvenile Justice*. New York: John Wiley, 1968.

Conrad, John P. "Crime and the Child." In *Major Issues in Juvenile Justice Information and Training: Readings in Public Policy*, edited by John C. Hall, Donna Martin Hamparian, John M. Pettibone, and Joseph L. White. Columbus, Ohio: Academy for Contemporary Problems, 1981, 179–192.

Croyle, James. "The Impact of Judge-made Policies: An Analysis of Research Strategies and an Application to Products Liability Doctrine." *Law and Society Review* 13(1979): 949–967.

Davis, Kenneth Culp. *Discretionary Justice*. Urbana: University of Illinois Press, 1969.

Doble, John and Mark Rovner. *A Qualitative Analysis of Public Opinion*. New York: The Public Agenda Foundation, 1986.

Drabek, Thomas, and Judith B. Chapman. "On Assessing Organizational Priorities: Concept and Method." *The Sociological Quarterly* 14(1973): 359–375.

Drabek, Thomas E., Alvin H. Mush Katel, and Thomas S. Kilijanek. *Earth-quake Mitigation Policy: The Experience of Two States*. Boulder, Colo.: University of Colorado, Institute of Behavioral Science, 1983.

Duffee, David E. *Explaining Criminal Justice; Community Theory and Criminal Justice Reform*. Cambridge, Mass.: Oelgeschlager, Grunn, and Hain, 1980.

Edna McConnell Clark Foundation. *Keeping Families Together: The Case for Family Preservation*. New York: Program For Children, 1985.

Eisenstein, James, and Herbert Jacob. *Felony Justice: An Organizational Analysis of Criminal Courts*. Boston: Little, Brown, 1977.

Emerson, Robert M. "Holistic Effects in Social Control Decision-Making." *Law and Society Review* 3(1983): 425–455.

Empey, LeMar T. *American Delinquency: Its Meaning and Construction*. Homewood, Ill.: Dorsey Press, 1982.

———. "Revolution and Counterrevolution: Current Trends in Juvenile Justice." In *Critical Issues in Juvenile Delinquency*, edited by David Schichor and Delos H. Kelly. Lexington, Mass.: Lexington Books, 1980, 157–181.

———. *Juvenile Justice: The Progressive Legacy and Current Reforms*. Charlottesville: University of Virginia Press, 1978.

Emrick, John, and Susan M. Peterson. *A Synthesis of Findings Across Five Recent Studies in Educational Dissemination and Change*. San Francisco: Far West Laboratory for Educational Research and Development, 1978.

Evan, William M. "The Organization Set: Toward a Theory of Interorganizational Relations." *Approaches to Organizational Design*, edited by James D. Thompson. Pittsburgh, Penn.: University of Pittsburgh Press, 1966, 173–188.

Fabricant, Michael. *Juveniles in the Family Courts*. Lexington, Mass.: Lexington Books, 1983.

Fairweather, George W., David H. Sanders, Louis G. Tornatzky, and Robert N. Harris, Jr. *Creating Change in Mental Health Organizations*. Elmsford, N.Y.: Pergamon, 1974.

Farace, Richard V., Peter R. Monge, and Hamish M. Russell. *Communicating and Organizing*. Reading, Mass.: Addison-Wesley, 1977.

Farrington, David P., Lloyd E. Ohlin, and James Q. Wilson. *Understanding and Controlling Crime: Toward a New Research Strategy*. New York: Springer-Gerlag, 1986.

Federal Bureau of Investigation. *Crime in the United States: Uniform Crime Reports 1982*. Washington, D.C.: United States Department of Justice, 1983.

Feeley, Malcolm M. "The Models of the Criminal Justice System." *Law and Society Review* 7(1973).

160 ———. *The Process is the Punishment: Handling Cases in a Lower Criminal Court.* New York: Russell Sage Foundation, 1979.

Feld, Barry C. "Juvenile Court Legislative Reform and the Serious Young Offender: Dismantling the 'Rehabilitative Ideal.'" *Minnesota Law Review* 65(1980).

———. Criminalizing Juvenile Justice: Rules of Procedure for the Juvenile Court." *Minnesota Law Review* 2(1984): 141–276.

Flicker, Barbara. "Prosecuting Juveniles as Adults: A Symptom of a Crisis in Juvenile Courts." In *Major Issues in Juvenile Justice Information and Training: Readings in Public Policy,* edited by John C. Hall, Donna Martin Hamparian, John M. Pettibone and Joseph White. Columbus, Ohio.: Academy for Contemporary Problems, 1981.

———. *Standards for Juvenile Justice: A Summary and Analysis.* Cambridge, Mass.: Ballinger, 1977.

Fox, Sanford J. "Juvenile Justice Reform: An Historical Perspective." *Sanford Law Review* 22(1970): 1187–1214.

Freedman, Samuel G. "As Young Unwed Parents Increase, Fathers Are Focus of New Attention." *New York Times* December 2, 1986: 14.

Fuchs, Victor R. *How We Live.* Cambridge, Mass.: Harvard University Press, 1983.

Galvin, Jim, and Ken Polk. "Juvenile Justice: Time for New Direction?" *Crime and Delinquency* (1983): 325–332.

Goldstein, Joseph, Anne Freud, and Albert Solnit. *Beyond the Best Interest of the Child.* New York: Free Press, 1973.

Greenwood, Peter W. and Franklin E. Zimring. *One More Chance: The Pursuit of Promising Intervention Strategies for Chronic Juvenile Offenders.* Santa Monica, Calif.: The Rand Corporation, May, 1985.

Hahn, Paul H. *The Juvenile Offender and the Law.* Cincinnati, Ohio: Anderson, 1984.

Hall, John C. "Introduction." In *Major Issues in Juvenile Justice Information and Training: Readings in Public Policy,* edited by John C. Hall, Donna Martin Hamparian, John M. Pettibone, and Joseph L. White. Columbus, Ohio: Academy for Contemporary Problems, 1981, 3–8.

Hall, Richard H., John P. Clark, Peggy C. Giordano, Paul V. Johnson, and Martha Van Roekel. "Patterns of Interorganizational Relationships." *Administrative Science Quarterly* 22(1975): 457–474.

Hamparian, Donna Martin, Richard Schuster, Simon Dinitz, and Joseph P. Conrad. *The Violent Few: A Study of Dangerous Juvenile Offenders.* Lexington, Mass.: Lexington Books, 1978.

Hannan, Michael T., and John Freeman. "The Population Ecology of Organizations." *American Journal of Sociology* 82(1977): 929–964. 161

Hasenfeld, Yeheskel. "People Processing Organizations." *American Sociological Review* 37(1972): 256–263.

Hasenfeld, Yeheskel, and Paul P. L. Cheung. "The Juvenile Court as a People-Processing Organization: A Political Economy Perspective." *American Journal of Sociology* 90(1985): 801–824.

Hawes, Joseph. *Children in Urban Society: Juvenile Delinquency in Nineteenth Century America.* New York: Oxford University Press, 1971.

Hechinger, Fred M. "Reform School Report." *New York Times* December 2, 1986: 21.

Horowitz, Donald L. *The Courts and Social Policy.* Washington, D.C.: The Brookings Institution, 1977.

Hutchins, Robert M. "Foreword." In *Pursuing Justice for the Child*, edited by Margaret K. Rosenheim. Chicago: University of Chicago Press, 1976.

Institute for Court Management. Unpublished materials from Workshop, Managing Cases in Juvenile Courts, June 22–25, 1986, Snowmass, Colo. Denver, Colo: Institute for Court Management, 1986.

Ito, Jeanne A. "Measuring the Performance for Different Types of Juvenile Courts." Williamsburg, Va.: National Center for State Courts, 1984.

Jacobs, David. "Dependency and Vulnerability: An Exchange Approach to the Control of Organizations." *Administrative Justice Quarterly* 19(1974): 45–59.

Jacobs, Mark D. "The End of Liberalism in the Administration of Social Casework." Unpublished presentation at the Annual Meetings of the American Sociological Association, Washington, D.C., 1985.

Jones, Robert E. "Productivity and the Structure of the Strategic Decision Process." Paper presented at the Western Social Science Association, Denver, Colo. 1982.

Julian, Joseph and William Kornblum. *Social Problems*, 5th ed. Englewood Cliffs, N.J.: Prentice-Hall, 1986.

Katkin, Daniel. "Foreword." In *Discretion and Lawlessness: Compliance in the Juvenile Court*, by James T. Sprowls. Lexington, Mass.: Lexington Books, 1980.

Ketcham, Oram. "The Unfulfilled Promise of the Juvenile Court." In *Justice for the Child: The Juvenile Court in Transition*, edited by Margaret Rosenheim. Glencoe, Ill.: Free Press, 1961.

162   Klein, Malcolm W., ed. *Western Systems of Juvenile Justice*. Beverly Hills: Sage Publications, 1984.

Kohlberg, L., and R. B. Kramer. "Continuities and Discontinuities in Childhood and Adult Moral Development." *Human Development* 12(1969): 93.

Krisberg, Barry, and James Austin. *The Children of Ishmael: Critical Perspectives on Juvenile Justice*. Palo Alto: Mayfield Publishing, 1978.

Law Enforcement Assistance Administration. *Indexed Legislative History of the Juvenile Justice and Delinquency Prevention Act of 1974*. Washington D.C.: U.S. Government Printing Office, 1974.

Lawson, Harry O., and Barbara J. Gletne. "Cutback Management in the Judicial Branch: Controlling Costs Without Courting Disaster." *The Justice System Journal* 71(1982): 44–69.

League of Women Voters. *A Citizen's Guide to Children's Laws*. 1979.

Lemert, Edwin M. "The Juvenile Court: Quest and Realities." In *Juvenile Justice and Youth Crime, President's Commission on Law Enforcement and Administration of Justice Task Force Report*. Washington, D.C.: U.S. Government Printing Office, 1967, 91–106.

———. *Social Action and Legal Change: Revolution Within the Juvenile Court*. Chicago: Aldine, 1970.

Levin, Mark M., and Rosemary C. Sarri. *Juvenile Delinquency: A Comparative Analysis of Legal Codes in the United States*. Ann Arbor, Mich.: National Assessment of Juvenile Corrections, University of Michigan, 1974.

Levin, Martin. "Delay in Five Criminal Courts." *Journal of Legal Studies* 4(1975).

Lincoln, Yvonna S. "The Substance of the Emergent Paradigm: Implications for Researchers." In *Organizational Theory and Inquiry: The Paradigm Revolution*, edited by Yvonna S. Lincoln. Beverly Hills: Sage Publications, 1985.

Lindsey, Ben. "The Juvenile Court in Denver." In *Children's Courts in the United States*, edited by S. Borrows. Washington, D.C.: U.S. Government Printing Office, 1904.

Lundman, Richard J. *Prevention and Control of Juvenile Delinquency*. New York: Oxford University Press, 1984.

Luskin, Mary Lee. "Analyzing Case Processing Time in Criminal Cases." National Institute of Justice, U.S. Department of Justice, 1981.

Luskin, Mary Lee, and Robert C. Luskin. "Case Processing Time: Issues of Explanation and Reform." Unpublished Report, Indiana University, Bloomington, Ind., 1984.

Macaulay, Stewart. "Lawyers and Consumer Protection Law." *Law and Society Review* 14(1979): 115–171.

McCarthy, Francis. "Delinquency Disposition Under the Juvenile Justice Standards: The Consequences of a Change in Rationale." *New York University Law Review* 52(1977): 1093–1119.

McNally, Roger B. "Juvenile Court: An Endangered Species." *Federal Probation* (1983): 32–36.

Magnetti, Susan S. "Effects of the Education for All Handicapped Children Act on the Deinstitutionalization of Status Offenders." In *Neither Angels nor Thieves*, edited by Joel F. Handler and Julie Zatz. Washington, D.C.: National Academy Press, 1982, 699–722.

Mahoney, Anne Rankin. "Nonresident Delinquents: Whose Problem Are They?" *Journal of Juvenile Law* 10(1986).

———. "Control of Delinquency: Can We Learn From The Past?" *Contemporary Psychology* 31 (1986b): 279.

———. "Time and Process in Juvenile Court." *The Justice System Journal* 10(1985a): 37–55.

———. "Jury Trials for Juveniles: Right or Ritual?" *Justice Quarterly* 2(1985b): 553–565.

———. "PINS and Parents." In *Beyond Control: Status Offenders in the Juvenile Court*, edited by L. Teitelbaum and A. Gough. Cambridge, Mass.: Ballinger, 1977, 161–177.

Mahoney, Anne Rankin and Carol Fenster. "The Effect of Legal Representation on Case Outcome and Processing Time in Juvenile Court." Unpublished Paper. University of Denver, Denver, Colo., 1987.

Mahoney, Barry, Larry L. Sipes, and Jeanne A. Ito. *Implementing Delay Reduction and Delay Prevention Programs in Urban Trial Courts: Preliminary Findings from Current Research*. Williamsburg, Va.: National Center for State Courts, 1985.

Mahoney, Barry, and Larry L. Sipes. "Using Time Standards and Management Information to Help Diagnose and Remedy Trial Court Delay." *Court Management Journal* (1985): 9–13.

Mahoney, Barry, Philip B. Winberry, and Thomas W. Church, Jr. "Addressing Problems of Delay in Limited Jurisdiction Courts: A Report on Research in Britain." *The Justice System Journal* 6(1981): 44.

Manning, P. K. "Queries Concerning the Decision-Making Approach to Police Research." Paper presented to the British Psychological Society, 1983.

Melcher, Frederic G. "Setting Time Standards: How Much Delay Is Too Much?" *The Judge's Journal* 23(1984).

Mennel, Robert. *Thorns and Thistles*. Hanover: The University of New Hampshire Press, 1973.

Meyer, John W., and Brian Rowan. "Institutionalized Organizations: Formal

164   Structure as Myth and Ceremony." *American Journal of Sociology* 83(1977): 340.

Mileski, Maureen. "Courtroom Encounters: An Observational Study of a Lower Criminal Court." *Law and Society Review* 5(May, 1971).

Mohr, Laurence B. "Organizations, Decisions and Courts." *Law and Society Review* 10(1976): 621.

Moran, J. Denis. "Stating the Case for Timely Justice." *State Court Journal* 8(1984).

Morash, Merry, ed. *Implementing Criminal Justice Policies: Common Problems and Their Sources.* Beverly Hills: Sage Publications, 1982.

Murray, Charles A., and Louis A. Cox. *Beyond Probation: Juvenile Corrections and the Chronic Delinquent.* Beverly Hills: Sage Publications, 1979.

Murray, Kay C. *Personal Communication* (November, 1986).

National Advisory Commission on Criminal Justice Standards and Goals. *Juvenile Justice and Delinquency Prevention Report.* Washington, D.C.: U.S. Government Printing Office, 1976.

National Center for Health Statistics, Department of Health and Human Services. Washington, D.C.: U.S. Government Printing Office, 1985.

National Center for State Courts. *Study of Structural Characteristics, Policies and Operational Procedures in Metropolitan Juvenile Courts.* Williamsburg, Va.: NCSC, 1982.

———. "Delay in Juvenile, Family and Domestic Relations Courts." *State Court Journal* 9(1985): 29–30.

National Task Force to Develop Standards and Goals for Juvenile Justice and Delinquency Prevention. *Jurisdiction: Status Offenders.* Washington, D.C.: National Institute for Juvenile Justice and Delinquency Prevention, 1977.

Needleman, Carolyn. "Discrepant Assumptions in Empirical Research: The Case of Juvenile Court Screening." *Social Problems* 28(1981): 247.

Nejelski, Paul. "Juvenile Justice in the United States." In *Youth Crime and Juvenile Justice: International Perspectives.* New York: Praeger, 1977.

Neubauer, David W., Marcia Lipetz, Mary Lee Luskin, and John Paul Ryan. *Managing the Pace of Justice: An Evaluation of LEAA's Court Delay-Reduction Programs.* Chicago: American Judicature Society, 1980.

Nimmer, Raymond. *The Nature of System Change: Reform Impact in the Criminal Courts.* Chicago: American Bar Association, 1978.

Ohlin, Lloyd. "The Future of Juvenile Justice Policy and Research." *Crime and Delinquency* (1983): 463–472.

O'Kelly, Charlotte and Larry S. Carney. *Women and Men in Society.* Belmont, Calif.: Wadsworth Publishing Company, 1986.

Packer, Herbert. *The Limits of Criminal Sanction*. Stanford: Stanford University Press, 1968.

Perrow, C. "Disintegrating Social Sciences." *Phi Delta Kappan* 10(1982): 684–688.

Pettibone, John M. "Juvenile Court Services—Introduction." In *Major Issues in Juvenile Justice Information and Training: Readings in Public Policy*, edited by John C. Hall, Donna Martin Hamparian, John M. Pettibone, and Joseph L. White. Columbus, Ohio: Academy for Contemporary Problems, 1981, 381–388.

Pfeffer, Jeffrey, and Gerald Salancik. *The External Control of Organizations*. New York: Harper and Row, 1978.

Platt, Anthony. *The Child Savers: The Invention of Delinquency*. Chicago: University of Chicago Press, 1969.

Platt, Anthony, and Ruth Friedman. "The Limits of Advocacy: Occupational Hazards in Juvenile Court." *University of Pennsylvania Law Review* 16(1968): 1156.

Polier, Hon. Justice Wise. "Myths and Realities in the Search for Juvenile Justice: A Statement by the Honorable Justice Wise Polier." *Harvard Educational Review* 44(1974): 112–124.

Pound, Roscoe. "Foreword." In *Social Treatment in Probation and Delinquency*, by Pauline Young. New York: McGraw-Hill, 1937.

———. "The Juvenile Court and the Law." *National Probation Association Yearbook* (1944): 1–22.

President's Commission on Law Enforcement and Administration of Justice. *The Challenge of Crime in a Free Society*. Washington D.C.: U.S. Government Printing Office, 1967.

Rothman, David. *Conscience and Convenience: The Asylum and Its Alternatives in Progressive America*. Boston: Little, Brown, 1980.

Rubin, H. Ted. *The Courts: Fulcrum of the Justice System*. New York: Random House, 1984.

Rutter, Michael. "Parent-Child Separation: Psychological Effects on the Children." *Journal of Child Psychology and Psychiatry* 12(1971): 233–260.

Ryerson, Ellen. *The Best Laid Plans: America's Juvenile Court Experiment*. New York: Hill and Wang, 1978.

Sarat, Austin. "Reexamining the Nature and Function of Trial Courts." Paper Presented at the Conference on Social Science Research on Courts, National Center for State Courts, Denver, January 20, 1977.

Sarri, Rosemary, and Yeheskel Hasenfeld, eds. *Brought to Justice? Juveniles, the*

166   *Courts and the Law.* Ann Arbor, Mich.: National Assessment of Juvenile Corrections, University of Michigan, 1976.

Scheirer, Mary Ann. *Program Implementation: The Organizational Context.* Beverly Hills: Sage Publications, 1981.

Schlossman, Stephen. *Love and the American Delinquent: The Theory and Practice of "Progressive" Justice, 1825–1920.* Chicago: University of Chicago Press, 1977.

Schultz, J. Lawrence. "The Cycle of Juvenile Court History." *Crime and Delinquency* October(1973): 457–76.

Schultz, J. Lawrence, and Fred Cohen. "Isolationism in Juvenile Court Jurisprudence." In *Pursuing Justice for the Child,* edited by Margaret K. Rosenheim. Chicago: University of Chicago Press, 1976.

Schur, Edwin M. *Radical Non-Intervention.* Englewood Cliffs, N.J.: Prentice-Hall, 1973.

Schwartz, P., and J. Ogilvy. *The Emergent Paradigm: Changing Patterns of Thoughts and Belief.* Menlo Park, Calif.: SRI International, 1979.

Schweinhart, L. J. and D. P. Weikart. *Young Children Grow Up: The Effects of the Perry Preschool Program on Youths Through Age 15.* Ypsilanti, Mich.: High/Scope, 1980.

Scott, Richard. *Organizations: Rational, Natural and Open Systems.* Englewood Cliffs, N.J.: Prentice-Hall, 1981.

Shichor, David. "Historical and Current Trends in American Juvenile Justice." *Juvenile and Family Court Journal* August(1983): 62–75.

Sipes, Larry L. "The Journey Toward Delay Reduction: A Traveller's Report." *State Court Journal* 5(1982).

Smith, Louis M., and Pat M. Keith. *Anatomy of Educational Innovation: An Organizational Analysis of an Elementary School.* New York: John Wiley, 1971.

Smith, Michael E. "Will the Real Alternatives Please Stand Up?" *New York University Review of Law and Social Change* 12(1983–84): 171–197.

Spencer, Gregory. *Projections of the Population of the United States, by Age, Sex, and Race: 1983–2080.* Washington, D.C.: U.S. Department of Commerce, May, 1984.

Spergel, Irving A. "Interactions Between Community Structure, Delinquency and Social Policy in the Inner City." In *The Juvenile Justice System,* edited by Malcolm W. Klein, Beverly Hills: Sage Publications, 1976, 55–99.

Sprowls, James T. *Discretion and Lawlessness: Compliance in the Juvenile Court.* Lexington, Mass.: Lexington Books, 1980.

Stapleton, W. Vaughn, David P. Aday, Jr., and Jeanne A. Ito. "An Empirical Typology of American Metropolitan Juvenile Courts." *American Journal of Sociology* 88(1982): 549–564.

Stapleton, W. Vaughn, and Lee E. Teitlebaum. *In Defense of Youth: A Study of Counsel in American Juvenile Courts.* New York: Russell Sage Foundation, 1972.

Starbuck, W. H. "Organizations as Action Generators." *American Sociological Review* 48(1983): 91–102.

Stone, O. M. "Children Without a Satisfactory Home—A Gap Family Law Must Fill." *The Modern Law Review* 33(1970): 649–661.

Studt, Eliot. "The Client's Image of the Juvenile Court." In *Justice for the Child*, edited by Margaret Rosenheim. Glencoe, Ill.: Free Press, 1961.

Stull, Barbara D. "Speedy Trial Rights for Florida's Juveniles: A Survey of Recent Interpretations by Florida Courts." *Nova Law Journal* 6(1982): 437.

Sturz, Elizabeth Lyttleton. *Widening Circles.* New York: Mentor, 1983.

(SYP) Suburban Youth Project. Unpublished Field Notes, 1976–1983.

(SYPN) Suburban Youth Project Newspaper Files, 1976–1983.

Sutton, John R. "The Juvenile Court and Social Welfare: Dynamics of Progressive Reform." *Law and Society Review* 1(1985): 107–145.

Tappan, Paul. *Delinquent Girls in Court.* New York: Columbia University Press, 1947.

Teilmann, Katherine S. "A Theory to Predict the Implementation of Reform Legislation." Unpublished paper. Los Angeles: University of Southern California, 1980.

Teilmann, Katherine S., and Malcolm W. Klein. "Juvenile Justice Legislation: A Framework for Evaluation." In *Critical Issues in Juvenile Delinquency*, edited by David Shichor and Delos H. Kelly. Lexington, Mass.: Lexington Books, 1980, 27–44.

Thompson, James D. *Organizations in Action.* New York: McGraw-Hill, 1967.

Thornberry, Terence. "Race, Socioeconomic Status, and Sentencing in the Juvenile Justice System." *Journal of Criminal Law and Criminology* 64(1973): 90–98.

United Nations. *Report Prepared by the Secretariat.* New York: United Nations, 1961.

Van Horn, Carl E., and Donald S. Van Meter. "The Implementation of Intergovermental Policy." In *Policy Studies Review Annual*, edited by Stuart S. Nagel. Beverly Hills: Sage Publications, 1977.

Vinter, Robert D., George Downs, and John Hall. *Juvenile Corrections in the States; Residential Programs and Deinstitutionalization.* National Assessment of Juvenile Corrections. Ann Arbor, Mich.: University of Michigan, 1975.

168 Wadlington, Walter, Charles H. Whitebread, and Samuel M. Davis. *Cases and Materials on Children in the Legal System.* Mineola, N.Y.: The Foundation Press, 1983.

Waegel, William B. "Case Routinization in Investigative Police Work." *Social Problems* 28(1981): 263.

Walker, Daniel. *Toward A Functioning Federalism.* Cambridge, Mass.: Winthrop Publishers, 1981.

Walters, R., R. Park, and V. Cane. "Timing of Punishment and the Observation of Consequences to Others as Determinants of Response Inhibition." *Journal of Experimental Child Psychology* 2(1965).

Wamsley, Gary L., and Mayer N. Zald. *The Political Economy of Public Organizations.* Lexington, Mass.: Heath & Co., 1973.

Wasby, Stephen L. *The Impact of the United States Supreme Court.* Homewood, Ill.: Dorsey Press, 1970.

Weick, Karl E. "Sources of Order in Under-Organized Systems: Themes in Recent Organizational Theory." In *Organizational Theory and Inquiry: The Paradigm Revolution,* edited by Yvonna S. Lincoln. Beverly Hills: Sage Publications, 1985, 106–136.

————. "Educational Organizations as Loosely Coupled Systems." *Administrative Science Quarterly* 21(1976): 1–19.

West, Donald J. and D. P. Farrington. *Who Becomes Delinquent?* London: Heinemann Educational, 1973.

White House Conference on Child Health and Protection. *The Delinquent Child.* New York: Century, 1932.

Wolfgang, Marvin E., Robert M. Figlio, and Thorsten Sellin. *Delinquency in a Birth Cohort.* Chicago: The University of Chicago Press, 1972.

Zald, Mayer N. "Political Economy: A Framework for Comparative Analysis." *Power in Organizations,* edited by Mayer N. Zald. Nashville: Vanderbilt University Press, 1970, 221–261.

Index